Whitey's Legacy

The crime-thriller sequel to *Goldmaker*
by award-winning author

Jim Hughes

This is a work of fiction. All characters, organizations, and events portrayed in this novel are either products of the author's imagination or are used fictitiously.

For information regarding permission, please write to:
info@barringerpublishing.com
Barringer Publishing, Naples, Florida
www.barringerpublishing.com

Design and layout by Linda S. Duider
Cape Coral, Florida

ISBN: 978-1-954396-45-6
Library of Congress Cataloging-in-Publication Data
Whitey's Legacy / Jim Hughes

Printed in U.S.A.

Thanks to Marshall for telling me to write it; for Anne who told me to write more of it; and, as always, for Eleanor who is my rock of support.

The Present

Chapter One

Boston

Mackie rolled over to the shrill ring and grabbed the phone, glancing at her clock.

"Yeah, who the hell is this? It's one o'clock in the morning! And the damn thing is on time out. It's not supposed to ring!"

"Ms. Mackie, this is the Attorney General . . ."

"Yeah, and I'm the Prime Minister."

"No, really Ms. Mackie, this is John Fenton, the new attorney general. I need to talk to you . . ."

"Okay, I'll play along. To what do I owe this honor?"

"You owe the honor to a problem we have down here in Washington over gold, Ms. Mackie. Does that ring a bell?"

She paused, thinking quickly about her adventures two years ago and the gold coins she had recently sent out. Now speaking softly, "Well, it's starting to ring, but not very loud." A deep sigh . . . "Well, maybe a little louder."

Jesus, what does the guy know? That I actually made some gold? That I sent those letters? And the coins? That I'm the new alchemist?

He continued, "I need to talk to you about what you've done."

"Go ahead, you woke me up, we're talking."

"No, I can't get into this on the phone, Mackie. We need to see you in Washington."

Maybe this is a hoax—the Israelis—trying to get me outside in the middle of the night. They tried to shoot me once. They warned me they'd come again if I made any more gold. What the hell do I do?

She stalled, "If you're really the attorney general, you got a bunch of cars outside my building and a bunch of suits at my door."

"We do."

"Shit," she muttered, rolling to her feet and padding to the window. Looking down from her third floor window, she saw two black SUVs idling at the curb. She then tiptoed to her front door and peered through the peephole. A bunch of people milling around the hallway outside her door.

Closing her eyes, she sighed and shook her head, *Probably need to open the door.*

She grabbed a robe, tied it tight and opened the door.

Two women stood there. Wearing dark suits, they were backed by some men in their dark suits. The taller woman addressed her, holding out her credentials.

"Ma'am, Ms. Mackie, we're from the Department of Justice and we're here to accompany you to Washington."

"Am I under arrest?"

"No, Ma'am. We've been told you're a very important witness who we need to get to Washington. But, no, no arrest—no compulsion. We're asking you to come voluntarily. Your choice. If you tell us to leave—we leave."

"And how are we going to get to Washington in the middle of the night?"

"We have a plane waiting, Ma'am," the agent responded. "It's in Bedford—we can be in DC first thing in the morning."

Mackie stared at the woman for a few seconds, then nodded, "I might not be under arrest, but I probably don't really have a choice, do I, agent . . . what's your name?"

"Smutthers, Ma'am, Elizabeth Smutthers."

"Okay, Agent Smutthers, let me get dressed and we'll go down to Washington. I need to first make a call, so why don't you wait in one of those nice cars you got downstairs. Give me thirty minutes."

"I'm told this is all pretty confidential, Ma'am, so I'm a little concerned about the phone call."

Mackie was starting to realize that she held a few cards. She crossed her arms and stared down at the agent.

"Look, Smutthers, you wake me up in the middle of the night and want to drag me to Washington. You say I'm not under arrest. If arrested, I'd have a right to make a phone call, right? I no longer work for you people. So, if I want to make a phone call, I'll make a phone call. Now leave me alone, I'll get ready, and I'll see you in thirty," pushing the door closed to end the discussion.

She walked back to the phone and grabbed it. "Okay, Mr. Attorney General, your people are here and I'll go with them. But you better get John Perkins to that meeting."

"Who?"

"If you wanna talk about gold, you better know who he is, and he better be there. Otherwise, it'll be a very short meeting, sir," hanging up. *That felt good. Hanging up on the Attorney General. He's the new boss.*

Mackie still had her Secret Service suits—black pants, matching black jacket—she got dressed and cleaned up. At almost six feet, slender, and black as her suit, she was an imposing young woman. She didn't wear makeup, other than a touch of light red lipstick. Kept her hair short. Since she worked out and ran, her legs were muscular and her shoulders broad. She was a tough woman, but an attractive one. Her only jewelry was usually some dangling earrings to help hide a scar from a childhood accident.

Once she was ready, she thought for a moment, then grabbed her cell phone to call her significant other, Jonathon Moore, a lawyer in Washington. She also pulled a folder from her desk drawer and slid it into her shoulder bag as she made the call. *I might need the report for this meeting. Telling everything I did with the federal task force in Florida—and everything John Perkins did. Wait, no signal. How can that be? I'm in the middle of Boston.* Frowning, she picked up her land line. *Dead also. But I just talked to the guy on it.* "Those sons of bitches," she murmured. "They killed my phones."

The Attorney General frowned as he hung up the phone. Turning to his aid, "Who the hell is John Perkins? I know I've only been here a month, but I don't think I've heard that name. Make some calls. Find out who he is, and we should try to get him here. We need her to talk, and it damn well can't be a short meeting."

Shaking his head, he muttered, "Don't know why we have to jump so high for the Israelis . . . I'm going home to get some sleep. Been a long day."

When Mackie reached the street, she saw Smutthers standing by one of the waiting cars. She walked to her and pointed her finger at the lady, "What the hell are you doing turning off my phones?"

The agent cocked her head and grimaced, raising her hands. "I didn't do anything to your phones, Ma'am. I did report that you were going to make a call, but that's it."

"Well, someone turned them off, and I'm not getting in this car or going anywhere with you if I can't make a call."

"I'll check," getting into the car and closing the door. In less than a minute, she got back out, saying, "I don't know how or why, but you might be right about the phone. I'm told it should work now."

Mackie stared back and shook her head. "I'll go back into the lobby and make my call. Don't know why I bother going inside, cause with all this shit, you're probably listening to it." Sure enough, the phone worked. She redialed Jonathon in Washington. It took a few rings, but he finally answered.

"Kate, that you? Something wrong? It's the middle of the night."

"No. Everything's okay, or sort of okay. I got the Justice Department at my door wanting to take me to Washington to talk to the new AG—Fenton, I think."

"No way. . . ."

"Yeah, they're here, with a plane waiting. They've obviously found out about my letters."

"Well, we knew they eventually would."

"But I didn't think they'd send a task force to arrest me in the middle of the night!"

"You're under arrest?"

"No, they say I'm not, but it feels that way. They're *asking* me to fly to Washington—that it's voluntary. Voluntary my ass."

"What are you going to do, Kate?"

"I told'em I'd go—sooner or later I gotta deal with this. Might as well get it over with."

"Why don't I get you a lawyer to meet you there, Kate. You need some protection, and it can't be me. I'm too close to the situation."

Mackie paused, clenched her jaw before answering, "No, I'll go alone. I've done everything else alone. But I told them to get Perkins there. I'm not going down and taking a hit for that son of a bitch. Sorry I woke you, but I had to talk to someone, and you're really all I have. I'll call as soon as this meeting's over tomorrow morning—whoops, I guess it's later this morning. They're waiting for me. Gotta run. Love you."

"Wait a minute, Kate. Just stop. Think a moment. I, I think you need to tell them everything. Don't hold anything back. You did nothing wrong. Don't try to protect people. Tell it all."

"Yeah. That's what I'm planning. I'm taking my full report—the one they haven't seen yet. I'll probably give it to them. Gotta get it off my chest. Has everything in it. From when the Secret Service first assigned me to the task force to find the gold counterfeiter; CIA's John Perkins running the group; Mossad's involvement; and our eventual success in finding and stopping the professor in Fort Meyers. A few things in between, too, like when they tried to kill me and when they tried to recruit the professor to make gold for the good old USA. It's all there. Most of them will be surprised—maybe more than surprised."

The plane, a small Pilatus, was sitting at the Bedford airport, a commuter airstrip just west of

Boston. She and Smutthers climbed the steps and the other agents drove away. They were soon speeding down the runway and airborne. Mackie finally turned to the agent with a tight smile, "Guess I can't blame you for just doing your job. We can probably be civil—talk to each other."

"That's what it is, Ma'am, my job . . ."

"You can call me Kate."

"I'm Beth, Kate. Understand you did some big things in the Secret Service."

"Yeah, I did some stuff in the Service. From counterfeiting to a special task force, to presidential protection. Started out when I met then President Menton while I was with the US Marshals. She brought me into the Secret Service, and it all took off from there. I think some of it might be coming back to haunt me now, though."

"Presidential Protection! That's heavy stuff. I seem to be mostly shuffling papers and, now, being an escort."

"Don't complain too much about the simple stuff, Beth. The line they fed you about me being a witness is bullshit. I've had foreigners and our own people try to kill me, and although they probably aren't about to kill me in Washington, I'll be walking a pretty narrow plank. It'll be hard not to fall off. . . ." Shaking her head,

"But I really can't talk any more about it Beth. Or they probably would shoot me."

Smutthers sat back in shock. She'd been told this was a simple transport. *Who the hell is this?*

Kate sat back with her own thoughts. She knew the flight would be short—less than two hours—and she was too hyped to sleep. So, she thought back about her topsy turvy life since she'd joined the US Marshals ten years before. Since then, she seemed to have one wild adventure after another. Always on the edge. She just couldn't sit back and let events control her. She had to take charge. She often wondered why.

Guess it started when I was bussed to that white school in South Boston twenty-five years ago with the other black kids. The streets were lined with an angry mob of whites yelling hate and holding signs saying, "Go Home!" and, "We Don't Want You Here!" Then they started throwing things at the bus. Rotten fruit, paint balloons, and then rocks. I got cut with flying glass, but I refused to go back. Even as a kid I was stubborn. I marched right off the bus and into the school with blood running down my face. Didn't say a damn thing. Didn't give an inch. Just went to school. "Guess that's still me," she murmured as they descended to Reagan International. *But why am I back in Boston? In an apartment halfway between that old school in Southie and the new Federal courthouse, the court that put me on the bus. Where else could I go? Certainly, wasn't going to stay in Washington with all those bad memories, even though Jonathon is there. They say Boston's changed. Hope so.*

"What'd you say?" asked Smutthers, turning to her.

"Oh, nothing. Just thinking out loud. Let's go do this."

Chapter Two

Washington D.C.

By seven a.m. they were in the back seat of a limo pulling up to the Department of Justice on Pennsylvania Avenue. Mackie hadn't been in the building before, since the Secret Service reported to Homeland Security rather than Justice, although she knew that the Department of Justice had a large say in what happened at the Secret Service. Indeed, the old Attorney General had been canned two years ago when her world came crashing down. So now she was apparently going to meet the new guy—this guy Fenton. *How much did he know?*

A small elevator took them to the top floor. Smutthers then delivered her to another agent—a man this time—who stood next to a door marked, *Private Conference Room, restricted access.* "Guess this is as far as I go, Ma'am. I've been told to wait to take you back to Boston after your meeting."

Kate nodded, "Thanks, but I have a few friends down here, and I might decide to stay overnight. I'll see how the meeting goes."

"I'll be here," Smutthers responded.

The new agent opened the door without a word and gestured her in. A big room—no windows she noted—with a large, polished conference table running down the center. There was one other door at the far corner, and she saw one chair was already filled. Her old boss, Bill McLaughlin, head of Presidential Security, sat with his hands clasped on the table and a grim look on his face. They'd had a good relationship when she worked for him. He spoke first.

"Hello, Kate. Thanks for agreeing to come."

She smiled and shrugged, "Sort of like an invitation I didn't think I could refuse, Bill. Glad you're here." She raised her eyebrows and tilted her head, "I hope we're in agreement on what happened."

He nodded and raised his hands, "Don't worry, Kate. I'm on your side, at least as much as I can be. I do wish you'd told me about your letters . . ."

He was interrupted as the corner door opened and three men walked in. McLaughlin stood to make introductions. "Mr. Attorney General," raising his hand to the third trailing man and sweeping it toward Mackie, "this is Kathryn Mackie, formerly with my team." The man walked to Mackie, extending his hand, "Miss Mackie, glad you're here. These," pointing to the two other men, "are my assistants." No names were given. *Looks like Mutt and Jeff—a six footer and five-foot-six—bet the taller one's in charge.*

"Have a seat, Mackie. Let's get started," pointing a finger at the assistant who carried a folder. "We want to show you some documents—letters, or notes, or whatever you want to call them—which we think you sent out to several people a couple of months ago, after you retired but dealing with your work before you retired. The Secretary of State has received a formal complaint from the State of Israel about these letters. Claims the United States is interfering in Israeli domestic affairs in violation of international law." Gesturing again to the same assistant, "Give her the letters."

"I know the letters, sir. I did send them, but it was two years after I retired . . ."

"Bullshit, Mackie. They deal with matters you were involved with before you left the Service," he snapped. "And you signed confidentiality agreements promising to keep all information confidential. What the hell were you doing?!"

Mackie swiveled her eyes around the room, "I don't see John Perkins, sir."

"No, you don't. I've learned there is a John Perkins with another agency, and I've also been told he's not available and knows nothing about these letters."

"Well, sir, John Perkins is a senior operative with the CIA. He ran the secret, and probably unlawful, domestic operation which caused me to send the letters. That's why the CIA director, and your predecessor Attorney General Abbott, resigned so suddenly a couple of years ago." The attorney general started to interject, but Mackie raised her hand to silence him, "No, let me finish. You dragged me here. Let me finish my story." She was still standing, took a deep breath, and sat with her arms crossed on the table.

"You know why Abbott resigned, sir?"

"Never gave it much thought," Fenton answered. "That was two years ago."

"He resigned 'cause he'd ordered me to conduct a secret program to make gold to compete with the Israelis who were already doing it," she spat. "When the President learned what was going on, he fired him, along with the CIA director. Abbott was in bed with the Israelis. And you tell me that Israel is now complaining and caused me to be dragged down here? The Israelis know damn well what happened since they had their own agent on the task force I was assigned to. They tried to kill me to assure my silence. I recently sent these letters to protect myself. So, I'm not too impressed by their feigned complaint about interference."

"What do you mean, they tried to kill you? Are you in touch with reality, Mackie? Are you making this stuff up?"

She turned to McLaughlin, "Okay, Bill, now's your turn. Who was the target at Faneuil Hall in Boston two years ago when a shot was fired at the Vice President's car?"

Still in his seat, the Secret Service chief fidgeted and swallowed before speaking, "You know, Kathryn, we never got the shooter, so we don't know for sure . . ."

"Cut the bullshit, Bill. Why was I assigned to office duty after the shooting?"

He nodded, "We certainly recognized that you might have been the target, Kate. Didn't quite add up that the shot missed you by inches while the Vice President was still in the car." Holding his hands up in exasperation, "But we didn't know for sure. Still don't. You're right we reassigned you just in case you were the target. Couldn't have even a possible target protecting the Vice President. And, yes, your previous assignment had probably put you at risk."

"And talking about Vice President Roberts," added Mackie in a now calmer voice, "who's now announced for the Presidency, with an unusual pro Israel platform, he was involved in this stuff up to his ears."

"What the hell is this all about?" shouted the attorney general, turning beet red. "A domestic CIA operation? An Israeli involvement? An assassination attempt? And Vice President Roberts involved?" He was sputtering.

Mackie stared at him with a set face, "It's about an operation in South Florida that I was assigned to while in the Secret Service. To find a person who was making fake gold—a counterfeiter if you will. We found him, we stopped him, but in the process we uncovered some inconvenient facts. Inconvenient to the CIA, to Israel, to Cuba, and to a few others up here in Washington. If you really want the full story, here it is," pulling a sheaf of papers from her case and dropping them on the table. "That's my report. It's all there. The whole story. No one has seen it up till now but me. And, as I told John Perkins, a copy of this document is held by a secure source with directions that it should be released if I'm killed or attacked. It's probably all that's kept me alive these last couple of years."

She took a breath, "The letters you've seen were simply heads-up anonymous notes I sent to several investigative journalists around the world, suggesting they might want to look into Israeli's gold coins. I enclosed a coin with each letter, which, if analyzed carefully, would turn out to be a very realistic copy but slightly off in weight. The letters don't divulge much at all—they were intended just to get their attention. They simply said, 'You should look into this.' Nothing more; nothing less. I did not identify myself. Don't know whether any of them have done anything with the story. But since the Israelis sent you after me, someone must be asking some questions, and they're probably pretty sure I sent them."

"How many did you send out," the attorney general asked in a now much quieter voice.

"Close to a hundred," Mackie answered, "and each one with one of the new Israeli coins they call Jerusalem of Gold. At least my version of it."

One of the assistants—the shorter one—pulled out a calculator and hit some numbers, "That would have cost you almost a hundred thousand dollars to get those coins!"

She smiled and looked down for a second, saying softly, "I didn't exactly buy them."

"You stole them?"

"No, sir." She shook her head." "I made them."

The Past

Chapter Three

South Boston

About 1980

Sean Aiden unlocked and pulled open the front door of his art gallery on East 2nd Street in South Boston at his usual 11 a.m. *Aiden's Gallery,* announced the plaque over the door. His gallery. *And maybe a bit of an albatross around my neck,* he thought, flipping the door sign from Closed to Open and picking up the few pieces of mail on the floor. He walked to his small desk in the rear. His dream upon immigrating from Belfast—from The Troubles—had been to have his own shop. Irish art in the Irish enclave of South Boston. He'd opened his shop, then discovered the Irish in Southie already had their history—they didn't need much more from the old country. So his customers—

the few that he had—were often those in the suburbs who liked to pretend to be Irish.

The Troubles had hit his family hard in Belfast. As a Catholic, he'd faced armed and masked IRA soldiers on street corners and barricaded streets many nights. His parents often just cowered at home. It was no place to raise a family. So, with his parents' blessings, he took his wife and baby, Tommy, and fled to South Boston. He knew it wouldn't be a perfect place, but at least his family would be safe there, he thought.

South Boston was a three square mile neighborhood on Boston's south side which had not yet grown beyond the projects and the underwhelming three deckers built in the '40s and long before. About thirty thousand people jammed into that small area. Pretty much all white. Many on public assistance. Many on the public payroll. And mostly all were of Irish descent.

Still in his twenties, Aiden was slight of build and looked a bit like a leprechaun, with tufts of red hair surrounding his thinning hair on the top. He claimed five feet six in height; maybe a little exaggeration. Although not himself much of an artist, he worked hard to bring in art from his old country for people to enjoy. He was married to Rosemary and still had one son.

He heard the bell jingle as, hopefully, one of those customers from the suburbs walked in. *Don't think so,* he thought, as he watched the man enter.

Aiden saw a middle-aged man with hands in his pockets slide through the door and look around the small store. The man wore chinos and a sweatshirt. Not six feet, and slim, thinning blond hair, he sort of sauntered as he walked toward the back desk.

"You Sean? Aiden? The owner here?"

"Yes, sir, that's me. Best pieces from Northern Ireland you can find in Southie." He had detected traces of Irish brogue beneath the man's brusque questions.

"Might be the best, but I hear you're not selling much of it," the stranger shot back.

Holding back a stinging retort, Sean remained polite, "I'm doing okay, sir. What can I do for you?"

"Might be what I can do for you, Aiden," the man growled. "Help the business a bit. Make each of us a little money."

"And you are who, sir, who's going to help me so much?"

"They call me Whitey," he answered with a tight grin showing his discolored teeth. "I live right down the street, as does my family and my friends."

"Whitey . . . ?" raising his hands and shoulders to ask the rest of the name.

"Whitey's enough." He stepped closer, looked around as if to make sure they were alone, "Let's talk a little business," pausing so close that Sean could smell his tobacco breath. "I got some Irish art I wanna sell—nothing really special—but could be worth a lot to the right person. I need someone to sell it—an assignment, I think they call it."

"You probably mean, a consignment," Sean said.

"Yeah, whatever . . . I bring it to you, you sell it, and I let you keep five percent."

"Well, Whitey, that's a little low for a consignment. Usually calls for a fifty, fifty split. You know, I have to advertise, hold it, take the risk of it not selling . . ."

"No," the man interrupted, shaking his head, "it'll sell—right away—it'll sell real quick."

"And how are we going to sell it, "real quick?"

"Cause I'm going to buy it back. Sort of like washing my linen—my Irish linen," he chuckled. "I give you cash and get a nice clean check back from you and you get five percent for doing nothing."

Aiden finally realized what was going on and, all of a sudden, he also realized who this guy was. Whitey Bulger, well-known local mobster. He had heard the guy ran betting and extortion throughout South Boston. Rumor was that Whitey was violent. He also knew he was in trouble. "Sounds like I might be breaking the law."

"Don't worry about the law, Mr. Sean. I got that covered."

"And if I say, no?"

Whitey backed up and nodded as he looked Sean up and down.

"That would be a problem, Sean, that would be a big problem. I'm looking to do you a favor here. Helping you make some money. I think you and your nice family should see this as a neighbor helping a neighbor." Staring at him, "Never refuse to help a neighbor."

"Can I think about it—maybe talk to my wife?"

"You think about it as much as you want, Sean, but I don't want you talking to no wife. This is a private deal between you and me—between you and Whitey. Think as much as you want," turning to head out of the shop while adding over his shoulder,

"We'll have the first assignment here tomorrow."

The Present

Chapter Four

Washington Dinner

"So, what'd they say after you told them you'd made the gold coins?" Jonathon asked. He and Kate sipped wine in a booth at Clyde's at the end of her day at the Department of Justice. They had first met while she was assigned to presidential protection. He was a lawyer with a large DC firm. They met while jogging, she managing to beat him to the finish line—he claiming he was a gentleman and having slowed down. He wore glasses and looked a little bookish, equal to her in height. Theirs had been an on again off again relationship for over three years. Now it was back on.

She drank her wine and looked at him over the glass.

"I think they almost shit their pants. Suddenly calculator agent—who I knew by then was in charge—

was scurrying about and escorting the AG out, saying they appreciated my help but had other appointments; that they'd review the documents and make some phone calls; that we'd all regroup in a couple of hours. He told the other guy—called him Chet—the tall one—to grab my report off the table and take care of me. Suddenly, he was in a great hurry. Chet was actually quite nice. He said we'd resume at eleven and he'd send in coffee and something to eat. Knew it had been a long night for me. Told me a bathroom was right outside their exit door. I did ask him if my phone would work. He said, sure, our phones work here. He picked up my report from the table and left."

"So, they left you alone?"

"Yeah. The guy who had brought me into the room had not stayed. I was alone."

"What'd you do?"

Mackie laughed quietly, taking some more wine.

"Well, I was suspicious, and curious, so I tiptoed over to the door I came in through and tried the handle. Sure enough, it was locked. Then I started to tiptoe back to the table but realized I was probably on camera and mike. So, I just went and sat down. Pretty soon someone did bring in some coffee and rolls and juice. I had my phone; it worked; so, I relaxed and did some stuff and waited. Think I nodded off. It had been a long night."

"And did they come back?"

"Oh, yeah, at least some of them. Right at eleven, calculator man and Chet reappeared, but no Attorney General."

"And what'd they have to say?"

"You want to hear it, or read it?" Mackie answered as she pulled her phone from her bag and put it on the table.

"What do you mean?" Jonathon asked with raised eyebrows.

"I thought it might be a good idea to have a record of what was said—sort of like I did two years ago when the AG ordered me to make gold. So, I put my phone on record, and it has a transcription feature which I enabled. So, I have their voices and a transcript of what was said. Actually, it was only the shorter calculator man who did all the talking. Chet was there, but I don't think he said anything. I kept the phone in my bag, so they didn't know they were being recorded."

"Jesus, Kate, you think of everything. Might be an illegal recording, but at least you have it. Too public to play it here, but let me look at the transcript."

"Sure." She picked up the phone, tapped a few buttons, and put it back on the table in front of Jonathon. The screen was small, so he picked it up to read the conversation.

"We're still working on this, Miss Mackie. You've made some pretty serious allegations against some pretty important people. Our office is looking into them and making some calls. It's going to take us a few more hours to even begin to understand what happened here, so we want you to stay here a while longer while we touch some more bases—talk to some of these people."

"What if I choose to leave?"

"That would be a mistake, Mackie. At the least, your report makes you a material witness to a whole bunch of shit—and a participant in some of it. If you want, I can get the FBI over here to detain you, but I think it's in your interest to just stay put while we try to get to the bottom of this. One way or the other, we're going to try to wrap it up today." He hesitated a moment, then added, "But we do have one important question. Do you have any other copies of your report?"

"The only other copy is, as I said before, being held by a secure source. You try to make me a scapegoat—it'll be released to the press."

"And who is that source?"

"I'm not going to tell you that, sir."

The screen then went blank. Jonathon looked up at Kate, "What happened?"

She chuckled, "I think someone finally realized that I still had my phone and had been using it. So, they shut it down, like they had done up in Boston. So that's all I have recorded. The conversation pretty much ended then, anyway. I told them I'd wait a few more hours, but I would be leaving after that, so they could bring on the FBI if they wanted to."

"I wasn't too pleased to have been dragged down to Washington."

Taking a full gulp of her wine and waving for another glass, "I guess I sort of lost it. Told them they were a bunch of assholes, and what the hell did they think they were doing dragging me out of bed in the middle of the night; that they were a bunch of storm troopers, as well as assholes." She smiled at Jonathon, "Probably not one of my better moments. But I was pissed."

The second glass was delivered and she stared at it for a moment, "Probably a good thing that wasn't recorded."

"They then left me alone again, and good old Chet brought in some sandwiches and stuff. My phone wasn't working, so it was pretty boring. Finally, about two o'clock, I think, all three of them came back into the room. This time, AG Fenton did the talking. Said much of my report appeared to be accurate but that some of it was definitely being challenged. In particular, he said that the Vice President vehemently denied any involvement in any gold-making scheme and would—I think his words were—come after me like a ton of bricks—if I made that claim in public. He reminded me that Roberts was running for the Presidency and should probably not be taken lightly. As for the Israelis, he said they had withdrawn their complaint, saying it had been issued in error. I remember his closing words."

"Miss Mackie, we want this matter closed. We'll get you back to Boston. Your report will remain confidential, and we expect you to treat it the same. Let's all forget about the gold. And, for God's sake, don't try to make any more."

"I didn't really say much after that. It was clear they were back-tracking big time and wishing they hadn't opened this can of worms. Told them to unlock the door and let me leave; that I'd get back to Boston on my own. Once my phone was back on, I called you," lowering her head and frowning, "it was a tough day." She then perked up and smiled, "but I'm okay now . . . Wait . . . there's more . . . some good news. I got a message from my headhunter in Boston—she has a possible position for me. An interview with a local museum—The Isabella Stewart Gardner Museum."

"What do you know about museums, Kate?"

"Not much. But it's for chief security officer. I do know a little bit about security."

She reached over and held his hand, "Now let's forget about today and focus on tonight. . . . You still have room for me at your place?"

"You know I do."

"Then let's do take out and go to your place," squeezing his hand.

Chapter Five

The Vice President and John Perkins

Later the Same Day

Vice President Roberts showed his age and forty years of rough and tumble politics in Texas and Washington. Still with a full mane of silver hair, almost a requirement for aging politicians, he was heavy set and six feet tall. He had helped Texas and other conservative-leaning states to elect the more progressive president. Now in a fight for the Republican Presidential nomination, he was trembling with rage as he confronted John Perkins in a parlor room at the Vice Presidential residence.

"I get a call from some fucking assistant to the President, asking about some Secret Service Agent

Mackie and gold! What's going on, Perkins? This was supposedly all put to bed two years ago!"

"It'll be okay, sir. For some reason Mackie got dragged down to the Justice Department and asked about her work on the Florida task force. She gave them some sort of report which mentioned a meeting with you . . ."

"Well, I goddamned told them no such meeting ever happened!" Roberts thundered. "She was the one on my protection detail who almost got shot in Boston couple of years ago. So, I told them sure, I knew her and talked to her from time to time, but never about any fucking gold!"

Perkins could smell the liquor on the man's breath, so he kept his answer simple.

"That's fine, sir. There's no record of any such meeting, and Justice is not going anywhere with this. I think the Israelis screwed up and made some sort of diplomatic protest about Mackie. They've now withdrawn the protest. I think the matter is closed."

"I don't want you to "think" it's closed, Perkins. You make goddamned sure it's closed. And you let Mackie know she's treading on thin ice if she keeps this shit up."

"I plan to talk to her, sir. Soon. I'll make it clear to her that your name is not to be mentioned by her again. I'm confident she'll agree."

Calmed by the reassurances, the Vice President continued.

"Look, John, I'm running to help make peace in the Middle East. My plan for Israel to become our fifty-first state is not as crazy as some claim. Israel's not much farther from Washington than Hawaii. All it takes is a vote of Congress. Those Arab bastards won't attack Israel if it's a state!" Then, smiling and continuing in a whisper, "And, don't forget, John, they'd bring some gold to the table."

He waved his hand to end the discussion, "I can't get derailed by Mackie."

The Past

Chapter Six

South Boston—
Day After Whitey's Visit

About 1980

The night after Whitey's visit, Aiden asked some friends about this guy, Whitey Bulger.

"Bad news," he was told. "Life of crime here in Boston. I heard he spent some time in Alcatraz for a bank robbery years ago. Ever since, he's been doing mob stuff here in Boston—mostly in Southie. Why? Why you wanna know about him?"

"Just wondering," Aiden answered. "Heard he had a lot of money. Maybe I could sell him some art."

"Stay away from that guy," the other friend said. He'd just as soon kill you as talk to you. He's running the numbers, the horses, everything. Yeah, he has plenty of money. But you don't want to do business with him. And guess what? His brother Billy's in the damn State Senate and runs the place."

The next morning, Aiden thought about staying home, keeping the shop closed, but they knew where he lived, where his family was. Maybe they wouldn't show up, maybe the visit had just been a bad dream. So, true to form, he walked into his shop late morning. Not much happened till early afternoon.

The bell tinkled as the day before, but the visitor was someone new—a kid, actually. In his twenties, dressed like a slob.

"Mr. Aiden?" he asked as he walked through the store.

"Yes, that's me," he said standing up from his desk. He saw the kid was carrying a large paper bag.

"Got a delivery for you, sir. Some paintings I guess. Think you're supposed to sell them."

"Let me have a look," Aiden said as he took the bag and opened it. His heart fell. "This is junk!" he exclaimed, pulling out the cheap prints that were in the bag. About a dozen—typical Irish scenes of sheep on green hillsides and small, thatch-roofed cottages. "I can't sell this stuff! At least not for more than a few bucks."

"Hey, I just deliver the stuff," the kid said, raising his arms and shrugging. "I just deliver the stuff, come back tomorrow with the cash, and the next day for a check."

"But no one's going to pay anything for these . . . pictures," pointing at the bag's contents.

"Hey, all I know is it's usually a pretty big bag of cash I bring back . . ."

"You mean you've done this before?"

"Sure. We got a few guys like you who help us out." Pausing, "I'm told this is your first delivery, so maybe you don't know how it works." He pulled a slip of paper from his pocket, reading it, "looks like you're going to get fifteen thousand tomorrow—you can count it when I bring it in—and then the next day, I pick up a check, less your five percent. They write down all the numbers for me. The check should be payable to L Street Enterprises. "

"Here," handing Aiden the slip he was reading from, "it's all on here."

God, what have I gotten myself into, thought Sean.

"Well, well . . . I need a taxpayer ID number, and I'm not sure the bank will give me a check for that much cash without a bunch of paperwork." *Maybe that's the way out. The bank won't go along.*

"No worry, sir. We got the bank all lined up. Go over to South Boston Savings down the street—make sure you go to that one. Ask for Billy Flynn, the manager. He'll take care of everything."

Sean shook his head as he put down the bag. "And I guess you'll want the check in a bag?"

"No, sir," sounding confused. "An envelope's fine. The bank will give you one. And, just so you know, I'm Billy, some call me Billy Bags—but just Billy is fine. Look's like we'll be seeing a lot of each other."

The Present

Chapter Seven

Gardner Museum Interview

Back in Boston, two days after her trip to Washington, Kate prepared for her interview by going online to learn a bit about the museum. In Boston's Back Bay, the Gardner Museum had been built and filled with mostly European art by Isabella Stewart Gardner, a millionaire heiress, in the early twentieth century. A big addition had been added a hundred years later. Originally modeled after an Italian palazzo, with dark rooms and heavy drapes and all types of art displayed throughout its rooms, the new addition was sheathed in glass and added a modern theme. Classrooms and a theatre had been added, joining the new to the old. What surprised Kate, however, was the attention the website gave—not to the art—but to a theft of the art.

She read that on the night of March 17/18, 1990, St. Patrick's Day weekend, a small group of thieves entered the museum and stole some of its most important pieces of art. And, amazingly, they were never caught. None of the art had ever been recovered. That story and its aftermath received almost as much attention on the site as the museum itself. Now, thirty years later, the crime remained unsolved. The stolen art still unrecovered.

"Ms. Mackie, I really am glad to meet you. I'm Marilyn Ketchum, director of the museum." Kate had just walked into Ketchum's top floor office at the museum.

She responded, "Glad to be here, Ma'am, and thank you for bringing me in so quickly." She had read that Ketchum had walked away from a senior position in the financial world in Boston—with a ton of money—to take this job. She'd been director of 'the Gardner'—as it was known—for about three years.

"Well, Kate, with your resume, not to speak of your recommendations, I decided to move quickly. Sometimes even museums can do that," she chuckled. "As for the recommendations, did you know I have one from the Secret Service director, one from the head of the US Marshal's, and," looking down to read, "as of this morning, one from the United States Attorney General? Oh, and let's not forget former President Menton. What in the world have you done to get all these people to recommend you?"

If you only knew, Kate thought, *especially calling the AG an asshole. He must really want me to stay quiet.*

Then answering, "With the Marshals, and the Secret Service, I was put into some challenging situations, and I was lucky enough to handle them well. As a US Marshall, I worked an assignment that put me in touch with then President Menton. She liked what I did and pulled some strings to get me into the Secret Service." Shrugging her shoulders, "Pulling the strings got me in the door, but I had to pull my own weight after that. I'm usually able to keep up with the guys. That's about all I can really say."

"You mean you'd have to shoot me if you told me more?" Ketchum smiled.

Smiling back, "Secret Service agents only shoot as a last resort, Ma'am, so that certainly wouldn't be my first choice."

"But my real question, Ms. Mackie. Why did such a high performer suddenly quit and end up here in Boston in the job market?"

"That's pretty easy, Ma'am. As for Boston, I grew up here. Not much family still around, but I grew up in Dorchester. Went to school pretty much across the street," pointing over her shoulder, "Northeastern." She paused, as if to think, "Why'd I leave the government? And then the private security company Xe after the last two years? That's a tougher question, and both were tough decisions. But I have a close relationship with a man I hope to marry—we're talking about it—and we want to raise a family and lead the traditional American life. I don't think we could have done that if I had stayed in the Secret Service, or in a similar position at Xe. I was with the government for seven years and then two years with the private company. I saw a lot of marriages fall apart and a lot of dreams destroyed. Just not very family-friendly careers. Lots of travel; lots of late nights with the guys. Just wasn't right for us. At Xe, I was basically a well-paid bodyguard for mostly rich guys travelling around the world on business—sometimes government types. My heart wasn't really in it."

Hope she buys that—there's certainly some truth to it.

"Yes, I can understand that," looking down at Mackie's papers. "So, tell me a little about your experience with electronic security systems, crowd control, and theft prevention. Those are our main security concerns here at the museum."

For almost an hour they discussed electronic security systems and the current security operations at the museum.

Ketchum explained that the museum had recently hired a consultant to review its security systems. The conclusion was that they were uncoordinated and no one person appeared to be in charge. After the report—maybe as a result of it—the chief of security had resigned.

"So, we need to replace him, and to upgrade a bit. We've had too much petty pilfering and minor assaults and robberies. Mostly small stuff. But we want our patrons to be and feel safe. With our new wing, we have more and more high tech art. I'd like to see more high tech security."

"You've probably heard about our huge theft thirty years ago," Ketchum said. "Three Rembrandts, a Vermeer, Monet, Degas, the list goes on and on, taken in the middle of the night. Never recovered. Not a single one recovered. We can't let that happen again."

"And you put out a big reward, didn't you?"

"Yes, it was before my time—luckily—first a reward of a million, then raised to five million after a few years, and now since I've been here, it's been upped to ten million dollars. But no takers, at least no real takers—a few fake attempts at extortion. A part of your job description would be to keep the search alive, but a small part. We've pretty much given up hope that the art still exists."

"I'll be honest, Kate, or Kathryn?"

"Most call me Kate."

"Okay, Kate, let me be honest. I think you'd be perfect for the job. And, even though I shouldn't say so, it's nice you're a woman. Our security force is mostly men. Gotta work on that. But you need to talk to our HR director and take some tests, and I need to talk to my board and some others. So, I'll send you over to Pat McConnell in HR. I'll try to be back to you by end of day tomorrow—that okay? Not about to jump for something else? . . . I know, I'm not supposed to ask that question. Forget it."

"No problem, Ma'am. I'll also be honest. I don't have a lot of irons in the fire. I really never gave museum security a lot of thought. But protecting art's probably a lot like protecting the president—and, at least with art, it's not moving around all the time. And that theft intrigues me. Think it happened when I was a kid growing up here in Boston. I like to solve tough problems. That's what I'm trained to do. Who knows, maybe I could win the ten million dollar reward."

"We'd pay it gladly if you could, Kate. And, by the way, the reward does not exclude employees. Hopefully, we'll talk tomorrow."

The Past

Chapter Eight

Aiden's Journey

Sean Aiden did as he was told. As promised, banker Billy Flynn took care of everything—the consignment documents, the tax i.d.'s, all the paperwork.

"Mr. Aiden, that's why we're here—to take care of the details. Don't you worry about a thing," Flynn said as he sat behind a polished mahogany desk, smiling. "And what about your business account? Your personal account? Sean, can we do it better for you here?"

When he started the money laundering—because he knew that's what it really was—Aiden didn't know much about Whitey Bulger. As the years went by, he learned more. Bulger had a stranglehold on crime in South Boston. He took out the Italian mob by secretly partnering with some senior FBI agents and feeding them information about the Italians. He extorted from many of the local businesses—mostly bars—and there were a lot of them in Southie; he ran the betting and numbers lines; he got paid for protection. When he was crossed, people simply disappeared. He controlled the drug traffic in Southie by giving the dealers a simple choice—pay him a cut or be killed. Rumor was he enjoyed violence, sometimes being called "Boots," because of the switchblade he carried there.

Aiden also saw another side to Bulger—almost like he was looking out for the shop keeper. In one delivery bag, when he pulled out the contents, he was sure one was an oil by the famous Irish artist Paul Henry—a lush emerald landscape. Probably worth a fair amount. He told Billy Bags the painting was worth a lot more than the usual deliveries.

Next day Billy reported back that the boss said, "You can keep out whatever you want to sell yourself. Just sell us back the junk."

And then, another side. One delivery had prints which were splattered with stains. He pointed them out to Billy, who explained, "Sorry, Mr. Aiden. They were in the trunk with someone."

"Someone in the trunk?"

"Well, I don't think he was alive, but looks like some blood got on the stuff. Don't worry. We'll still buy it back. No problem."

Aiden tried to close his eyes to the bad. He didn't think Rosemary knew what was going on. She never spoke of it. But when she did the books, and looked at the deposits, she'd sometimes comment, "Another good consignment, Sean?"

"Yeah, a referral from the last one."

"Seem to be quite a few," she said once.

"You complaining?"

"No. But I guess I'm questioning."

"Don't worry. I'm building a network—getting known."

Eventually they just stopped talking about the growing number of consignments. The money was good, but they were both unsettled.

One thing she refused to do.

"It's your new bank, Sean."

"But it's our bank, Rose. They're doing a good job for us."

"Sean, they're a bunch of slime balls. That William Flynn oozes slime. You want to deal with him, fine, but I'm not going in there."

"Okay. I'll do the bank visits." *Probably better that way.*

A routine developed. Most Tuesdays (he worked the store alone on Tuesdays) Billy Bags, or his fill-in, came in with a bag of prints. As with the first delivery, they were usually worth very little. Aiden thought some of them had just been turned around and redelivered. He'd fill out an official looking consignment form describing the stuff as special Irish art. The following Wednesday, Billy would deliver a bag of cash and pick up the artwork. Aiden would then go to the bank to pick up a check, and, on Thursday, alone again, Sean would deliver the check to Billy Bags, less his five percent. He filed the consignment forms and receipts in case he was ever questioned. On the surface, they looked like normal art consignments and sales. His wife, Rosemary, helped out in the shop most Wednesdays, but he managed to keep her in the dark. His cut was seldom huge—usually about a thousand dollars—but it helped a lot. His business had been struggling, but as the months and then years, went by, the new cash cushion kept him going.

Then Southie started to change—gentrification they said—and the newcomers wanted to advertise their Irishness. They wanted Irish art for their newly renovated, three decker condos, so his legitimate business of selling real Irish art grew. He wasn't getting rich, but he was doing okay. Then, one day, another unexpected visitor, in a policeman's uniform, entered the store.

"Mr. Aiden?" Aiden nodded, trembling; scared.

The officer pointed his finger to the door. "Let's talk—outside." Sean nodded again and followed the policeman to the sidewalk.

"Mr. Aiden, we got a problem with your son. He's dealing drugs . . . to kids. We've been told to give you a heads up—don't know why but looks like someone's looking after you. You need to fix this, sir, or we'll fix it. We'll bring him in. We don't want drugs going to our kids." He stood stock still and stared down at Aiden. "You understand what I'm saying?"

"Yes, I hear what you're saying (*which is worse—a money launderer father or a druggie son?*), but I had no idea . . . I don't know what to say. He's only fifteen. This is . . . is a total surprise."

"Might be, Mr. Aiden, but you gotta fix it. And right away."

"Yes, officer. I'll talk to him right away . . . my wife and me this afternoon. I'll find out what's going on, and I'll stop it. Will you let me know if there're any more problems?"

"No way. You got a free pass on this one. Don't really know who you know. But no more freebees. You stop it or we will."

The officer turned and walked to a patrol car idling at the curb, got into the passenger side, and the car pulled away.

He called Rosemary right away, catching her at her part-time bookkeeping job.

"Rosemary, we have a problem—a big one."

"What is it?"

"The police were just here. They say Tommy's into drugs—that he's dealing drugs!"

"Has he been arrested?"

"No. This was sort of a warning . . . to tell us to fix it . . . or he will be arrested."

"Our Tommy? No, he wouldn't do that! Why'd the police come and talk to you? Isn't that a strange way of doing things?"

"I don't know, Rose, but we need to talk to him—do something—before they do arrest him."

Just then his shop door opened and Billy Bags walked in.

"I gotta go. Someone's here. Can't talk about this anymore, but get Tommy home right after school. I'll be there. We gotta fix this."

He looked up at Billy Bags, "Not the normal day, Billy. What's up?"

"Whitey needs to see you. Right away."

Haven't seen him since that first visit. Now, suddenly, can't be a coincidence.

"Sure, Billy. I'm alone in here now . . ."

"He said right away, Mr. Aiden. I think that means now."

"Oh . . . well, I guess I can lock up. Is he coming here?"

"No. He's over at Triple O's—his normal place. He wants to see you there."

Triple O's

Sean knew of the bar but had never been in it. On West Broadway across from the T station. The front room was a dark, drinking place, guys at the bar with their shots and chasers, even at eleven in the morning.

He was directed up the stairs to a large room. Whitey was standing with a few others next to a pool table. One of them was huge—must have been over three hundred pounds. Bulger waved them away as Sean approached. Aiden hadn't seen Whitey since that first meeting in his shop—more than ten years ago. The man had aged. Thinner hair, a growing paunch, but still looking sure of himself. He wasn't smiling today.

"Sean, what the fuck is your family doing?" he growled softly.

"Whaddya mean, Whitey?"

"Your son's in the drug business, bringing attention to our business, and as far as I know, he'll blow our entire deal! That's what I mean, asshole!"

"I really don't know much, sir, just got a visit from the police . . ."

"I know about the fucking visit. I set it up, and I had to pull in a few favors to do it. Now what the hell are you going to do?"

"Look, I've called my wife. We're going to talk to him this afternoon. We'll get to the bottom of it and stop whatever's going on. But it shouldn't have any effect on our business . . ."

"Are you fucking kidding me—he gets pinched and he probably squeals everything he knows about us."

"He doesn't know anything, Whitey. Even my wife doesn't know. I've kept it all very quiet."

"Yeah, sure. You might be surprised how much a wife, or kid, or girlfriend knows about what's going on. And now the law's probably watching you. You've brought attention to us. I don't need attention! I got some problems around here, and I don't need any more fucking attention!"

"I'll stop whatever's going on. I promise. This afternoon."

"Look, Sean," turning his head, looking around to make sure they were alone, "the easiest thing for me to do would be to whack him . . ."

"Tommy's my son, Whitey!"

"I don't care if he's your fucking grandmother!" Standing straighter and looking serious, "I don't like to whack kids—against my principles—but I'm not going to let him bring me down." He crossed his arms and stared, "Do we understand each other, Sean?"

"Yes, sir. I understand. I'll take care of it—today."

"And, Sean, no more deliveries for a while. They might be watching your shop."

"Whatever you say, Whitey. Whatever you say."

Back Home

They sat Tommy down as soon as he got home from school.

From sullen silence turned to tears, he finally spoke, looking down and avoiding eye contact.

"Yeah, I've fooled around with some stuff. But nothing big. Nothing to really get all uptight about . . ."

"Don't get uptight!" Sean yelled. "About drugs—maybe selling them?"

"Not really, Dad, just foolin' around."

"You know of a guy named Whitey Bulger, Tommy?"

Shrugging, "I've heard of him."

"Well, he told me this afternoon he was going to kill you—he said whack you—if you don't stop. And the police also talked to me."

"How the heck do you know Whitey Bulger, Dad? He's a mobster."

"How I know him's not important. What's important is getting you out of drugs, off the street, and away from here before he decides to do something."

"Whaddya mean?"

"Mom and I think you need to go away to school—maybe just for a year—but we have to get you away from this guy. There's a very good academy in Ireland I know about. It's called the Villiers school—in Limerick. I've sold some stuff for them. Since you'd be full pay, they'll get you in. That's what I mean, Tommy. You'll go to school in Ireland for the rest of the year to get away from this mess."

After Tommy headed to his room, yelling that he hated them both, Sean's wife pulled him by the arm to the kitchen. "What's this about Whitey Bulger, Sean? Is he where the money's been coming from?"

"What do you mean?" he pleaded in a soft voice.

"I'm not stupid, Sean. I'm a bookkeeper, for God's sake. I've seen all that cash. And moving all the accounts to the new bank. I was just waiting for the day you would tell me what's going on. That's today, Sean. What . . . the . . . hell . . . is going on!"

He shrugged, took a long sigh, and explained.

"How could you do that to us! Put us in with the mob. He's . . . he's . . . a killer."

"That's why I did it, cause he's a killer. He threatened us all. He threatened you and Tommy!"

"Why didn't you go to the police?"

"You know he owns the police. He sent them to the store this morning to talk to me about Tommy. He owns everyone in Southie. Bottom line—he made me a proposal I couldn't really turn down. So, I made my pact with the devil."

"So, how long is this going to continue, Sean?"

"Well, it's on hold right now. He says we might be being watched—'cause of what Tommy's been doing. So, nothing more is going to happen for a while. And if I read him right, I think things are starting to go south for him. It might be close to over."

The Present

Chapter Nine

Mackie's Apartment

It was early evening before Kate returned to her apartment after the Gardner interviews. Late October, so it was dark in Boston. She had found an apartment in the Seaport District adjoining South Boston. On Berkeley Street—one bedroom on the third floor was all she really needed. She'd retired too early for much of a pension, but a lot of comp and vacation time had provided a pretty decent separation check. She'd had to spend a lot of it on furniture since she'd never really had to furnish a place. So it was sparse, but livable and comfortable. She was back to her Boston roots—although they were pretty shallow roots. An aunt and uncle and a few nieces were the only family she still had here.

She thought the Gardner interviews had gone pretty well. The HR tests were silly, searching her thinking for socially unacceptable thoughts and behavior. Nothing compared to the polygraphs and psychiatric evaluations she had undergone with the government. She wanted to get on the phone right away and talk to Jonathon.

Unlocking her door, she felt a little uneasy—just a quick tremor—before she hit the light switch. Everything looked fine. Then she saw him—the man in the chair. Gasping, she went to draw a weapon, but she no longer carried one.

"Don't be alarmed, Kate, it's only me."

"Goddamnit, Michael Bent, you gave me a heart attack! I could have shot you! Why the hell are you sneaking into my apartment?"

"I'd just as soon no one knows of my visit. And I knew you weren't still carrying a gun. Not here in Boston—the cradle of gun control. So, I let myself in. You might investigate some better locks, Kate. Wasn't that hard."

Michael Bent looked like the Israeli Mossad operative that he was. Not a big man—under six feet—lean and wiry. It was his eyes that set him off. They never blinked. Just stared right through you. He had been on the task force with Mackie in Florida two years earlier. Had set explosives to kill her—then warned her off. A conflicted guy, she had always thought.

"How'd the interviews go, Kate?"

"You bastard. You've been following me. What the hell's going on?"

"Well, Kate, we need to reach some closure after your session in Washington. We need to know what you told them. You tried to blow us out of the water with those letters of yours. And the coins—by the way—how'd you get the coins? You had promised not to make any more gold." He waited for an answer.

She was still standing, and now pointed a finger at him, "After you guys tried to shoot me at Faneuil Hall, I knew you weren't going to let me go . . ."

"Kate, you sent the letters a long time after Faneuil Hall."

"Well, maybe I did. Have you seen the letters? They said almost nothing. I sent one simple statement to a whole bunch of investigative reporters—"Simply said, 'You should look into this.' And I enclosed one of your coins. One of your new, Jerusalem of Gold fake gold coins. I thought you had to be stopped. Someone had to know Israel was making gold. I'm not sure if any of them did anything. Letters probably went in the trash. Hopefully not the coins."

"Why, Kate? Why does someone have to know, and why do we have to be stopped?"

"Because it's just not right! As Perkins explained to us in Florida, you can bring down the world financial system if you flood it with fake gold. You figured out how to make gold, and you're running a secret gold-making operation in the desert at Qumran."

"But we won't do that, Kate. We're only creating a supply in case there's a real Armageddon. Sort of like the weapons we don't talk about. We'll never talk about the gold, and we'll hopefully never have use it."

She continued, "Look, maybe we'll just agree to disagree. I didn't go all public. I just gave some reporters a tidbit of information if they wanted to pursue it. It looks to me like no one did. I'm not going to do anything more. Anyway, I gave all the information to the Department of Justice when I was down there. It's out of my hands. You can kill me, but you can't kill the entire Justice Department."

"No one's getting killed, Kate. But you've answered my main question. You say they know everything you knew?"

"Yes. Everything. My full report."

"Then we'll just have to deal with it. I'm sure we'll come up with some explanation about the gold. But there is one reporter asking quite a few questions. Faisal Al Hussein, of Al Jazeera. Was he one of the folks you sent the note to?"

"Michael, I'm not going to answer that. My role in this has ended. I want nothing further to do with it."

"So, getting back to my first question, Kate—How'd the interviews go? Are you employed again? In charge of museum security?"

She shook her head in amazement, finally sitting down.

"Went okay, I think. It'll be a little less stressful than what we did in Florida. And I don't think anyone'll be shooting at me."

"You going to solve that old Gardner Museum art theft as part of your job?"

"Who knows?" shrugging her shoulders. "It's not a big part of the job. But I'm going to look into it."

Bent pointed to the book on her coffee table—"You reading Silva's new book?"

"Yeah, Silva's pretty good. Are you guys really like his agent Gabriel Allon?"

The agent stroked his chin and stared at her before answering, "Maybe he's a bit too gentle."

"Easy to have a heart in fiction, Kate. Sometimes harder in real life." He stood to leave, "You know, Kate, maybe you should do what Gabriel did in the book? Do a counterfeit painting, to draw out the real ones."

She stared back at him, "I don't think the Gardner has a master art counterfeiter on its staff, Michael."

"I understand." He walked to her door and turned for one final comment, "As I said, real life is a bit harder than story telling." He gave a small wave, "Goodbye, Kate."

After he left, Mackie went to her laptop and pulled up the list of reporters she had contacted. Sure enough, Mr. Hussein of Al Jazeera's Washington office was on the list. *He must be pursuing the story,* she thought. *Need to warn him he might be in danger. They know he's looking into it. They know his name.*

She didn't want to use her phone, or her computer, because each could be traced back to her. There was an internet café on Commonwealth Avenue. The next day she went to the café and sent an anonymous email to Faisal Al Hussein at Al Jazeera: "Mr. Hussein, I am the sender of the previous note with the gold coin. The Israelis know you are looking into the matter. You could be in grave danger. Others have been killed. Please take all precautions and take care." She sighed as she signed off—*it was all she could do.*

Chapter Ten

The New Job

Kate got the job at the Gardner. First she needed to know what she was protecting, so she spent a week walking the floors and gardens, immersing herself in the recreated Venetian Palazzo and the more recent glass-sheathed addition. There were a lot of visitors—over three hundred thousand a year she was told.

She tweaked the security systems a bit, but she was smart enough not to do too much, too soon.

"What happens when we close?" she asked one of the security personnel.

"We lock the doors, Ma'am."

"What about a sweep?"

"Sweep?"

"You know, like a walk through to make sure no one's left inside."

"Well, I guess we could do that," he answered.

Asked another, "Those lockers, where people store their things. Are they scanned?"

The lady shook her head.

"Let's see if we can do that."

At the end of her first week, Kate met again with the director to give a quick report on her first impressions.

"Things look pretty good. I've changed a few things, but I think security is pretty tight—or at least as tight as it can be with three hundred thousand folks coming through the doors," she smiled. "I've checked all the sensors and cameras. I found a number aren't working, so I've scheduled repairs. Now, about that old robbery, are there some files and paperwork I can review to learn a little about it? I saw the empty frames in the galleries. Where the paintings were ripped out. They were startling."

"They look sad, don't they, Kate. Waiting for their paintings to return. Waiting for a long time. Guess it's our way of saying, we won't forget you."

She looked up, back to business, "As for files, we have plenty of files. More than you're going to want to read." She opened her drawer and pulled out some keys. "Have you been in the basement, yet?"

"I was down there yesterday—just briefly."

"Go down again, to the back, you'll see a wire mesh screen with a padlocked gate. I don't remember what the sign says. But there are a bunch of file cabinets in there with everything about the robbery—and I mean everything. Here's a key for the lock. It will take you forever to go through that paperwork, Kate."

"Don't worry, Marilyn, I won't let it take away from my real job. Probably do it on my own time—in the evenings," adding with a wry smile, "with my fiancée in Washington, I have plenty of time most evenings."

"That's your decision, Kate. Let me know if you solve the crime of the century. You know, they actually call it that. They say it's the single largest robbery in the history of the world—that the art taken was worth five hundred million dollars. Maybe more today. And, now, thirty years later, we don't have a single piece back."

Mackie found the file room—actually, a file cage, and started planning how she would attack the files. She called the art supply department, which was a pretty big operation to support the various classes and workshops run by the museum.

"Hi, this is Kate Mackie, new chief security officer. Yes, fine . . . thanks. Look, I need some supplies down in the basement in the cage where all the old files are kept . . . Yeah, I'm going to spend some time going over the files. What I need is a large table, and chair; a large bulletin board and chalkboard; flip charts, and stuff like tape, thumb tacks, chalk, paper, etcetera. Can you do that? . . . Great. . . . By tomorrow? . . . Great. Thanks for the help. The cage is locked. . . . Oh, okay, you can get in."

The Files

Mackie spent a week of evenings going through the files, in the basement right across from where the security guards had been tied up thirty years ago. The robbers—at least two—maybe more—had in some way entered through the museum's front, supposedly locked, doors just before midnight on Saturday, March 17, 1990. It was Saint Patrick's Day, a big weekend of celebration in Boston. They overpowered the two guards and hogtied them in the basement. Then, as motion detectors would later show, they spent almost three hours roaming the museum, taking what they wanted. Having cut the external alarm lines, they weren't worried about being disturbed. No one became aware of the theft until staff arrived for work in the morning and found the guards in the basement.

There had been thirteen works of art stolen—not all paintings—and thirty years ago the FBI had assembled a very professional looking portfolio showing each item with its dimensions and features. A separate page with a photograph of each piece of art. She took the pages out of one of the portfolios and soon had two rows of pictures pinned to her bulletin board in front of her new table. From the two large Rembrandts to the smallest of them all—a two inch square etching, also a Rembrandt. Eleven paintings/drawings; one piece of Chinese pottery; and a bronze eagle finial made an eclectic and disjointed collection, she thought, trying to find some rationale behind what had been taken.

She read the police reports, the witness statements, and the field reports from the various investigators. All under the watchful gaze of the fishermen in Rembrandt's Christ, sitting in the boat in *The Storm on the Sea of Galilee*—probably the most well-known and valuable of the stolen paintings. The painting greeted her when she walked in, and, alone when she left, probably missed all the patrons who had once gazed up at it.

To steal paintings, she understood. But why also a Chinese wine vessel and a bronze flagpole finial? She focused on those two pages and the information on them. Neither made any sense since neither appeared to have great value. *Were they a sort of diversion—to take attention away from the real goal? Or maybe these guys hadn't been as smart as thought. Maybe it was just a grab and run.* No matter how much she thought about it, she couldn't figure it out.

"Bronze flagpole eagle finial carried by Napoleon's First Regiment of Imperial Guard in the early eighteen hundreds," she murmured. "Ten inches high. Six and a half pounds.... Wait! How can a bronze finial—essentially a hollow bronze tube—even though in the shape of an eagle—weigh six pounds?" Made no sense. Had to be a typo. *But the FBI doesn't do typos.*

After a week, she had a pretty good idea what had happened back in March 1990, but very little idea why the theft remained unsolved. Someone would have to come up with a new approach—a new idea. She met again with the director.

"Just wanted to let you know that I've looked over the files, Ma'am."

"So, I've heard. Heard you've been burning a lot of midnight oil down in the basement," with a small smile.

"Well, they certainly did a thorough investigation. I think it's pretty clear that whoever stole these things is no longer around. By now, they're either old men or dead. I see the FBI thinks they're dead. I don't think anyone would have destroyed the art. I think someone got it from the robbers and has been sitting on it all these years. Probably the only way to get it back now is to give someone a reason—an incentive—to return it—obviously for money. So, I'm going to think about that for a while. See if I can come up with something... Oh, but one anomaly I saw in the paperwork. The Eagle finial—says it weighs over six pounds—that's impossible for a piece of bronze that size. I spent some time dealing with metal weights at the Secret Service. Bronze simply doesn't weigh that much."

The director stood, smiled broadly, and threw up her hands... "You've caught us, Kate! In thirty years, you're the first one who caught that."

"What?"

"It's not bronze, Kate. It's gold." She paused for a moment. "Right after the robbery, the FBI wanted to hold some information back from the press, and everyone else, to be able to test the veracity of anyone who came forward saying they had the art. And they were concerned that, if the robbers knew it was gold, they'd simply melt it down and sell the gold. So, yes, it was too heavy to be bronze. We lied about it. It was gold, Kate. Eighteen karat, if I remember correctly."

Mackie closed her eyes and thought before speaking, "Well, Ma'am, that puts an interesting new light on things. I know a lot about gold—things that I just can't get into right now. But, maybe I can come up with an idea or two. I just need to think about this new information."

"Whatever you say, Kate. I'm sure we'll talk about this again. But remember, we're telling everyone it's bronze. Don't give away our little secret."

"Don't worry, Ma'am. I can keep a secret."

The Past

Chapter Eleven

Aiden's Gallery— First FBI Visit

About 1990

A few months had passed with no art deliveries to Aiden's Gallery and no trips to the new bank. Tommy was away at school in Ireland, and Sean thought things were pretty much back to normal.

Two men in suits entered the gallery.

Aiden looked up with a small shudder. *Now what?"*

"Sean Aiden?"

"That's me."

"We're with the FBI, sir," the lead man said, holding out credentials. I'm Thomas Moran and this is Doug Purdy.

"Something wrong?"

"No. No. Everything's fine. We're part of a task force investigating the Gardner Museum theft. You know about that, don't you?"

Aiden closed his eyes in relief and breathed again. "Sure, I think everyone knows about it. Just a month ago, wasn't it?"

"That's right. We have a task force visiting every art store and gallery in the greater Boston area. We're trying to make sure none of this stolen art gets moved through any shops in the area."

"Well," answered Aiden with more confidence than he had a moment ago, "I haven't seen anything unusual. I'm not sure if I know exactly what was stolen."

"That's why we're here, sir." He handed a notebook to Sean, "We've put together a portfolio showing each item that was taken. Photographs and dimensions and all the details. We'll leave it with you. If you hear or see anything about anything in that notebook, we want to hear from you—right away. Names and numbers are there," pointing to the first page. "Why don't you look through it now. Let us know if you see anything?"

Aiden turned the pages—there were thirteen—and looked at each item, then said, "No, as I thought, nothing there that I've ever seen. I do recognize the Rembrandts—from art history you know—but nothing like that has ever come in here."

"Doesn't really surprise us sir, but we're talking to everyone. And don't be surprised if we come back. They're all over us on this thing. I think we'll be canvassing art dealers till we find something."

Turning to leave, "Thanks for your time, sir. I think there's another shop on our list—right down the street?"

"Yeah, half a block down—other side of the street."

Looking after them, *Jesus, that's all I needed. A visit from the fucking FBI.*

Chapter Twelve

Aiden's Gallery

A Few Years Later

There had been a few deliveries from Billy, but fewer and fewer. Aiden was actually relieved that most of his business was now straight forward art sales. Tommy was back in school locally. He had heard nothing further from Whitey Bulger, till he got a call.

"Sean?" His heart stopped—he remembered the voice.

"Yes, Whitey, it's Sean."

"Let's skip the names, okay?"

"Yeah, sure. What can I do for you?"

"I need to talk with you."

"About what?"

"Don't worry. It's not a problem—at least not one for you. You know Castle Island?"

"Yeah, sure."

"Meet you there in half an hour." He hung up.

A short drive to Castle Island, where he saw the man standing by the curb. It was Whitey Bulger, but a shadow of who he'd seen before. Now shrunken and bowed, looking old and uncertain. He pulled up next to him, and Whitey waved him to join him on the walkway.

"Let's take a walk out around the castle," he said. "Gotta be careful of these bastards. Got bugs, and wiretaps, and cameras, all over the place." They walked for a few minutes till he stopped, looked around, and announced, "We're probably okay here."

"Sure, Whitey. Whatever you say."

"Hey, we were pretty good for each other, weren't we? I saved your business—made you some money—you washed my dirty laundry."

"Yeah, I guess we helped each other, Whitey. But is it over? Can I stop being your laundryman?"

The now old man chuckled, pulling his pants up and standing straighter. "You wanna fuck with Whitey, Sean? You wanna piss him off?"

"No, sir. I just want to end it. Can we end it?"

"It's being ended, buddy. Not by me, or by us, but it's being ended. That's what I wanna talk to you about."

"Can I just go home, Whitey? Forget everything?"

"Not quite that easy, Sean . . . Our business is over, but I need one more favor—neighbor to neighbor—as they say."

"Please, Mr. Bulger, just leave me alone."

"I'm going to leave you alone, Sean." He folded his arms and looked straight at him, "Pretty soon, I'll be gone. Maybe shot; maybe arrested; maybe just disappeared. But I'm pretty sure I'll be gone. I need you to do something for me after I'm gone, cause I'm not sure I can trust anyone else."

"I was just your laundryman, Mr. Bulger."

"Yeah, but you were honest, Sean. You never cheated me, you sent your kid away when he became a problem, and you never squealed. That's important, Sean. You never squealed."

"What do I have to do now, Whitey?" raising his hands in supplication.

"One small favor, Sean. Here," handing Aiden an envelope. "I want you to hold this for me. Keep it safe and don't give it to anyone till the time's right. Put it away in your pocket right now," looking around.

"When will that be?"

"You'll know when the time's right. It's sort of a legacy—my legacy—Whitey's legacy. You'll know when the time's right."

"And who do I give it to?"

"Right now, I'm not sure, Sean, but legacies usually go to families. Just keep that in mind. I'm sure you'll make the right decision. Oh, and here's something for you"—passing over another envelope—"sort of a thank you thing. Remember, don't deposit more than ten grand at a time. The feds might see it."

"And, Sean, this here legacy is confidential between us—don't let anyone else know about it."

Two months later—in December 1994—Whitey Bulger disappeared. A week later, he was indicted by a federal grand jury in Boston for multiple crimes.

Aiden followed the search for Whitey Bulger on the news as the years passed. He read that the fugitive had been spotted across the country, and in Europe, but never apprehended. Always seemed to be one step ahead of the FBI. He had stored funds and identities in banks from Dallas, to Albuquerque, to New Orleans. Usually in safe deposit boxes. His corrupt FBI handlers—the main one being John Connolly in Boston—were arrested, tried, and convicted. Some of his associates also went to jail. But Whitey Bulger could not be found. As for his family, which he had referred to at the last Castle Island meeting, Aiden knew Whitey had two brothers. William Bulger was the long-term state senator from Southie, President of the Massachusetts State Senate, and later President of the University of Massachusetts. His brother John was the Clerk Magistrate for Southie's Juvenile Court.

Finally, in 2011, after almost twenty years, the media reported that Whitey Bulger had been located and arrested in Santa Monica, California. A tip from a hair salon customer had led to his girlfriend Catherine Greig and then to him. About eight hundred thousand dollars in cash was hidden in his apartment. The reports said there was probably much more secreted away in different locations.

He was returned to South Boston for trial. It was later learned that in 1994, he had been tipped by his friends at the FBI about the impending charges before he fled.

Chapter Thirteen

Whitey's Trial

2013

Aiden followed the trial in the *Boston Globe* and on TV. All the murders, the extortions, the police, and FBI on the take.

He hadn't really appreciated the extent of Bulger's depravity. Listening to the trial reports, he learned that the man had extorted hundreds of thousands from local businesses, sold drugs, and killed with impunity for over thirty years. Although the mobster had told Aiden that he had 'principles' against killing kids, he had strangled his girlfriend's young daughter simply because she had dropped his name too often.

Aiden held his breath as the trial went longer and longer, but he never heard mention of a small art gallery on Second Street which was laundering money for the man. For that he was grateful. But his curiosity finally got the better of him—he had to go down the street to the federal courthouse to see Whitey at his trial after all these years. What did the kingpin of Southie look like today?

He didn't get in on his first attempt—there were a lot of blood-thirsty folks trying to get a last view of the famous gangster.

The second day, Sean made the cut.

He watched as Whitey shuffled into the room with a court officer on each arm. He was now an old man, almost bald, stooped and hesitant as he walked. He fell into his seat next to his lawyer. Never really looked up. Too proud to recognize the powerlessness of his situation. There was a pad and pencil in front of him. He doodled constantly.

For some reason, just before a break, he did look up—over to where Sean Aiden sat. His eyes opened wide in recognition and made a little nod in his direction. That was all. Then he leaned over and whispered something in his lawyer's ear, nodding in Aiden's direction as he spoke.

At the break, Aiden went out into the hall to stretch his legs. As he walked, a man came up behind him and tapped him on the back.

"Mr. Aiden, sir? Mr. Sean Aiden?"

Sean turned—it was the lawyer.

"Yeah, that's me."

"I'm Whitey's lawyer, Mr. Aiden—Jay Carney—could I have a word with you?"

"I'd really rather not be at all involved with you, sir. I don't want anything to do with Whitey Bulger," and he kept walking.

"Just one question, Mr. Aiden. He asked me to ask you one question—actually wrote it down for me," looking down at a piece of paper in his hand.

"What's the question?"

Looking down and reading, the lawyer said, "He's asking, 'Is my legacy still intact?'"

Aiden stopped, sighed, and looked at Carney. He debated what to say, finally blurting, "You can tell him—yes—his legacy's still intact. But beyond that, I really don't want anything more to do with you."

He turned and left the courthouse. He had seen enough of the trial. Soon after, he read that Whitey had been convicted of eleven murders, extortion, money laundering, and narcotics distribution. He was fined millions and sent to prison for multiple life sentences in Florida. Luckily, however, the little art shop on Second Street had never been mentioned.

The Present

Chapter Fourteen

The Last FBI Visit

Agent Moran walked through the door, alone this time, greeting Aiden with a wave and short hello.

"Missed you these last few years, Agent Moran," responded shopkeeper Aiden. Aiden was now approaching sixty, fully bald, and although no longer a slight man, he wasn't yet portly. "Thought you were going to come by every March till you solved the Gardner thing—found the paintings."

"That's how I had it calendared, Mr. Aiden. To see you every anniversary of the theft till I got some useful information from you. Never got a thing from you. Missed the last two years cause of a bit of covid and my retirement—I'm actually a private citizen now, about to retire to Florida." Pausing, "This will be my last visit. How many times did I come in here? Ten?

Twenty? You never gave me anything." He crossed his arms and smiled at Sean.

"But now, with Whitey dead, thought you might be more willing to talk."

"Waddya you mean, Moran?"

"Come on, Sean, we knew you were in his pocket. You were laundering his cash for years with your fake art sales. We were told you were off limits—that he was a real special informant giving the feds lots of information." Shaking his head, "Turns out all he gave was cash, booze, and a girl or two, to his special friends."

"Well, I don't know anything about that. You don't think Whitey did the Gardner heist, do you? That's crazy."

"No, you're probably right, Sean. That job wasn't his style—too much planning and too complicated—he would have simply shot the guards. But in those days, Whitey Bulger owned Boston. In 1990, he was still the king around here. He knew everything that was going on. I guarantee he knew who pulled off that job. And I always thought you might know something. After all, you were his art guy."

"Interesting points, agent, but even if I might have sold a little Irish art for him over the years, I never, never, heard anything about the Gardner art or had anything to do with it."

"You sure he didn't get you to store it somewhere safe before he disappeared? Maybe he took it off the guys hands who couldn't sell it? Maybe he ended up with it even though he didn't steal it?"

"No way. I wouldn't have touched it with a ten-foot-pole, if he had asked. I really don't know anything about the Gardner stuff."

"What about that last meeting you had with him at Castle Island, Sean. Just before he disappeared. What was that all about?"

Sean looked startled,

"Jesus, you do know a lot, don't you, Moran." Pausing to think, "Yeah, he summoned me to that meeting. I think just to tell me that it was over. No more art sales. No more deals. Told me he might be leaving. Sort of like to say goodbye."

"Whitey Bulger didn't do goodbyes, Sean. Wasn't his style. He must have had something important to tell you."

"No. Nothing at all important. Next I heard, he'd disappeared. Never heard from him again. Then they finally found him. He got convicted right down the street"—pointing towards the federal courthouse—"I actually went to one day of the trial." Then they killed him, didn't they? Killed him in that prison in West Virginia, right? Why the hell was he in West Virginia?"

Moran had listened patiently, not believing a word of it, but knowing he had to leave it all behind. He was sure Sean Aiden knew more than he was saying. But it wasn't his job anymore.

"Wanna know why he was in West Virginia, Sean? Cause he'd decided to squeal some more. He'd decided he might get better treatment if he gave up some more people. He knew he'd never get out of prison, but he thought he might be able to improve his stay. West Virginia's a lot closer to Washington than Florida. Short three hour drive. So, he was moved up there to squeal to the feds."

"First I heard that, Moran."

"It's true, but no one wants to talk about it." He pointed at the art dealer, "Think he was going to give you up, Sean? Did he know something about you that was worth something? Maybe something about the Gardner art?"

"Look, Moran, I know nothing about the Gardner. Period. Amen. Now why don't you just go and enjoy your retirement. Maybe I'll see you in Florida if I ever retire."

After Moran left, Aiden sat and stared over at his small safe, which stood on the floor beneath an Irish tapestry. *What am I going to do with that envelope? His damn legacy. Should I open it? Give it to the FBI? Maybe just throw it away? I gotta at least see what's in it.*

First, the shopkeeper decided to learn more about Whitey's murder. He googled the subject and saw that there was a lot of information reported about the murder.

For some unexplained reason, the prisoner had been moved from his Florida prison to a facility in Oklahoma, and, then, on October 29, 2018, to the Hazelton Federal Penitentiary in West Virginia. He was put into the general prison population, which had been tipped that he was arriving.

That first night—October 29—three men entered his cell and beat him to death with a padlock in a sock. When he was found the next morning, his eyes had been cut out of their sockets, and, after he was dead, his tongue had been sliced off and yanked out of his mouth.

Aiden understood the tongue mutilation to be the age old penalty for an informer—a squealer. But the eye mutilation puzzled him. Almost like the man had been tortured for information. He continued to read the reports.

They said the Bureau of Prisons could not explain why he was transferred, how the transfer became known to the general prison population, or why he had been left unprotected.

The three killers were identified from prison video cameras and charged with the killing. Their leader was a mafia hit man from Springfield, Massachusetts, already serving a life sentence for murder. Rather than get assigned counsel, someone retained private attorneys to represent the three men. The reports said the charges were still pending.

As Aiden read, he realized that Moran's story about the transfer was probably right. Bulger had been moved to squeal, and he had been tortured for information and then punished for being an informer.

Chapter Fifteen

Jonathon's Visit to Boston

Kate was in the cage when her cell rang. She read the screen, "Jonathon! What a nice surprise."

"Where are you, Kate?"

"I'm spending this wonderful evening in my basement cage at the museum going over these damn interviews and looking at these damn pictures on the wall. All the art that was stolen. And I still can't figure it out! Why the mixture of very valuable paintings and antique heirlooms of little value."

"Need some help?"

"Whaddya you mean."

"I mean I'm coming to Boston tomorrow. Need to interview some witnesses in the morning, but my afternoon will be wide open. I will have to fly back tomorrow night."

"No overnight at my place?" she asked in a playful tone.

"Well, I will be there all afternoon . . ."

"Helping me review documents?"

"We can do that. Or whatever else comes to mind."

"Jonathon, this is wonderful! A wonderful break. You know where the museum is—call me when you get free and Uber over. I'll show you around—including my special basement cage office—and then we'll see what comes to mind, as you put it so gracefully. Can't wait!"

The next day, "So that's the grand tour, Jonathon. Right out of the Italian renaissance. Plucked from Europe and dropped right here in the middle of Boston."

They were standing in the Dutch room, before two large empty frames which exhibited only the wallpaper behind them.

"Very impressive, Kate. You're in charge of all this?" sweeping his arm around the area.

"Just the security. Trying to keep everyone and everything safe. A little bit like protecting the President—but much less pressure."

"And what about your basement cage office?"

"Oh, yeah, let's go down there. You can see what I've been up to most nights. And photographs of what was stolen." They took the elevator down two levels.

Pointing to the wire enclosure, "My cage."

Jonathon walked in and stood close to the bulletin board, looking from image to image, "Are these what they took?"

"Yep. Thirteen items. They're pretty impressive, aren't they?" She pointed, "That's Christ on the Galilee—look at him sitting calmly during the storm. And, Lady and Gentleman In Black—reminds me a bit of us. I guess we'd be in black and white."

He stood for a moment looking over the pictures. "What the hell did they want with a Chinese goblet—a . . . Gu? And the top of a flagpole—a . . . finial?"

"I'm still trying to figure that out, Jon."

He smiled and winked at her, "Hey, how about we go to your place? And I try to figure you out?"

"Then you jump a plane back to Boston?"

"Best I can do today, beautiful. You know I'd like to stay."

"Let's see your best, then," grabbing his hand and pulling him toward the elevator. "Yeah, let's go to my place and see your best," a twinkle in her eye.

Wine and love in the afternoon, left them lying side by side in Kate's bed. "Are we ever going to really tie the knot?" she murmured in his ear. "Really get married? Raise some kids?"

"We are, Kate. Now you have a secure job, and I think I'll soon make partner, so I think we're just about ready."

"Would ten million dollars help, Jon? Sort of like a dowry?"

"How about doing it tomorrow?"

"No, I'm serious. This robbery thing at the museum. There's a ten million dollar reward out there, and I've been told employees are not excluded."

"Well then go for it. As I said, you get ten million—I'll marry you tomorrow. Cause I'm in it for the money!"

"Oh, Jonathon, let's be serious. What color do you think they'll be—our kids?"

"I guess a little of each," pinching her, "since you're black and I'm white, I guess they'll be . . . gray?"

"You're impossible!" she laughed, pushing him out of the bed. "Go get dressed and catch your plane. I'm going back to the museum to catch some robbers! Although, after the wine, maybe I should stay right here and sleep it off. I think you got me drunk, Jonathon. And then took advantage of me!"

After he left, she did stay and dozed. And she dreamed:

> *She was walking in the Gardner central courtyard—lush with ivy, ferns, all hues of green. It was dark, and the air was heavy with a dripping fog. She was alone. In the middle of the garden the paths converged on a large, black kettle with two, three-legged easels beside it. Each easel held an empty frame, a matting but no picture. Two hands reached from the fog and grasped the kettle's handles—one from each side. And from the depth of the fog, she heard faint cries, "it's mine—no it's mine—it's mine, it's mine," the voices then fading away. In the middle of the pot stood a large, golden eagle.*

She woke with a start. Her shirt wet with sweat. She didn't usually dream. *What was that all about?*

Then she suddenly remembered Michael Bent's words before he left her apartment a month ago. "Make a fake to draw them out." She thought for a moment, then nodded.

That's exactly what she'd do. Maybe she couldn't counterfeit a great painting. But she sure as hell could make a golden eagle!

Chapter Sixteen

The Museum

Next Day

Kate got an appointment with Marilyn Kethum, the director, as soon as she could. She saw her at two o'clock.

"Ma'am, I need to follow up on our discussion about the theft—and about the finial."

"Seems to be taking a lot of your time, Kate. Maybe too much?" nodding and raising her eyebrows.

"No, I don't think so," pausing and taking a deep breath, "but I have an idea; a proposal if you will, that's going to sound very strange at first—maybe even outrageous. But if you'll listen, and if it works, we might be able to get that art back."

"Okay, Kate. I'm all ears—for this outrageous idea."

"Yes, well, the whole premise is that someone's sitting on the art. Waiting for the right time to give it up. The rewards haven't incented them to turn it over, and there's no sense to just keep raising the reward. We have to come up with something else—a new idea," pausing, "I want to play to their pride."

"Their pride?" Ketchum responded.

"Yes. If someone has the art, they're probably very proud of what they've pulled off. As you told me, the biggest robbery in the history of the world. These folks don't want to see someone else take credit for it."

"I think I'm following you . . ."

"I'm going to put together a scam operation that makes them think we're getting the art back from someone else, and, more importantly, going to pay the ten million dollar reward to someone else. I'm going to lure them out of hiding. Excuse the French, but I'm going to get them pissed off that someone else might claim to be responsible for the world's biggest robbery."

"And how are you going to do that, Kate?"

Mackie looked her straight in the eyes.

"I'm going to create a duplicate golden eagle that will pass all expert examinations. I'm going to announce it's been delivered to us as proof that they have the remaining art. That the rest of the art will be returned upon payment to them of a hell of a lot of money. We'll have a press conference, pictures, the whole shebang. Get a lot of publicity that the real robbers will have to see. They'll be bullshit thinking someone else is going to get credit and get paid. They'll contact us and say, "You got the wrong guy; you're being scammed. We have the real stuff. Deal with us."

"That is outrageous, Kate. Wildly outrageous. Puts us into the position of lying to a lot of people. I'm not sure the trustees would approve."

"We can't tell the trustees, Ma'am. This has to be held in a very tight circle for it to work. It's too easy for it to slip out."

"And how are you going to make a golden eagle, Kate. You told me, over six pounds, pure gold, and, as you said, it will be tested by experts. That's hundreds of thousands of dollars of gold. I'm sure you don't have that kind of money. I sure don't. The museum doesn't. How in the world would you get the gold?"

"Here's where you're going to have to have some faith and trust me, Ma'am," swallowing hard, "I can make the gold."

"You what!"

"I can make gold," Ma'am. "That was my last assignment at Secret Service. We caught a gold counterfeiter. It's a long story, and I can't really tell you the whole thing, but I learned the process. I learned how to make gold. And I actually made some. I think

I can do it again and duplicate the golden eagle finial. And no one will be able to tell it's fake. It'll be real gold."

"Oh my gosh! Young lady, you're going to give me a stroke. I can't believe I'm hearing all this. It's beyond me. I . . . I, just don't know what to say."

"I know it's a lot, and I've given this a lot of thought. With your permission, I'd like to reach out to the authorities in Washington who know about the gold. We can't do this without their assistance, and they can confirm to you that what I say is true. That I can make gold."

"And who would that be, Kate?"

"Probably the same guys who recommended me for this job—the Attorney General; the chief of the Secret Service; and, just to be balanced, former President Menton."

"Okay, sure. Talk to those folks. I'm not going to even think about authorizing this right now. But it doesn't hurt for you to talk to them and get their input. I'll need to hear from them also. It's a lot to think about." She started shuffling some papers to indicate that the meeting was over. Then she looked up, "Oh, the reward. I imagine you'd want the reward?"

"Obviously, I'm aware of it, Ma'am. But that's not my prime motivator. I'll do this whether I get the reward or not. Let's just leave the reward to another day."

Chapter Seventeen

Help from Washington

Mackie knew it was going to be tough to get help from Washington—she'd burned a few bridges down there. First thing in the morning, she called Jonathon to talk about it. She also had to tell him about the revelation by Ketchum that the eagle was gold. Jon knew about her background, and he knew how to keep a secret.

Before she made the call to Jonathon, she saw an incoming call from him.

"Good morning, Jon. I was just about to call you . . ."

"Good morning, Kate. Had to talk to you about some disturbing news I just read in the paper." He paused, then added, "What was that reporter's name at Al Jazeera who you tried to warn off?"

"Oh god," she said. "It was Hussein, Faisal Hussein I think. What happened?"

"Sounds like the same guy. He was mugged outside his office last night. Almost killed. It was late at night. The paper says they took his keys and entered his office, ransacked the place, and took all his files—took his computer." He paused for a moment, "Looks like the Israelis thought he was getting too close."

"Shit, Jon, I feel responsible. I tried to warn him. You said, almost killed; is he okay?"

"Sounds like he'll recover. He's in the hospital. Don't think there's anything we can do, but I knew you'd want to know. Sorry to start your day with bad news. So, you were about to call me?"

"Yeah, some developments up here at the museum. Much better news than yours." She then filled him in on the eagle being gold and her scheme to duplicate it and lure out the robbers.

"So that bronze finial turns out to be gold," he said, after listening to her story. "And you think you can use that against the robbers—use that unique skill of yours to make a golden eagle and draw them out?" He paused, "That gonna get us the reward? A nice wedding present?"

"Come on, Jon. I need you to be serious; I need your advice."

"I guess my advice is, you've got nothing to lose, Kate. Nothing else has worked. It's been thirty years. Worst that can happen is that the robbers—or whoever is holding the stuff—don't come forward. You're then stuck with a fake golden eagle. Melt it down and give it to charity. No one's out any money, and the museum comes up with some self-serving statement that they found it to be another fake extortion attempt to get the reward that failed. No damage done."

"You make it sound so simple . . ."

"Failure will be simple, Kate. It's success that's going to be difficult—very difficult."

"Let's work on success, Jon. Let's work real hard on success."

"Okay. First, you gotta get the FBI on board. You'll need them to police your scam and find and trace anyone who surfaces. And, unfortunately, you're not going to get the FBI interested by talking about alchemy—about making gold. Just put that completely out of your vocabulary."

"And, so how am I going to get the gold, Jon?"

"Well, of course, you're going to make it. You're just not going to tell them that. They don't need to know where the damn gold's coming from. Tell 'em you got a friend at Fort Knox! . . . pausing again, "No, seriously, all they need to know is that you're going to get some gold and forge a flag finial. After all, you're a museum. You probably got all kinds of gold in that museum."

"But we still have to get them on board."

"Yeah, that's the problem." Another pause, then, "How much did you piss Fenton off—the new AG?"

"He gave me a good recommendation for this job. And, if he read my report, which I'm sure he did, he knows I did a pretty good job at Secret Service and then got hung out to dry."

Jonathon spoke, "The FBI works for Fenton. Let's try to go through Fenton to get the feds involved. Use your buddy, Bill McLaughlin, at the Secret Service. He was at your meeting with Fenton—probably still has the hots for you—see if he can set up a meeting. But other than that, I gotta go. And, remember, Kate, go light on the alchemy stuff."

She decided to hold off calling McLaughlin while she first figured out one thing that was nagging her.

How was she going to make an exact replica of the finial even if she got some gold? She couldn't carve the damn thing. The photos were good, but not good enough for a replica that would pass a close examination. She decided to go to work, sit in her cage, and see if she could come up with an idea. Maybe she'd get an inspiration from Rembrandt's *Christ*, or the artist himself in his *Portrait as a Young Man*, or the singer at Vermeer's *Concert*. After all, they were all there, in her cage, waiting for her.

Chapter Eighteen

Making an Eagle

It turned out to be so easy. As she sat in the cage, she figured she might as well look in the cardboard boxes stored in the corner. There were three of them, all marked Gift Store. She had ignored them up till now because the gift store upstairs had nothing to do with the robbery. Two of them were stuffed with old prints and old memorabilia which had evidently once been sold in the store. The third, however, contained a bonanza. A dozen or so plastic eagle finials, painted gold, which appeared to be close copies of the stolen one shown in the picture on her board. The gift shop had evidently sold these copies as inexpensive mementos. Would have been years ago, she figured based upon the thick layer of dust on the box. She hadn't seen them in the gift shop.

She pulled one out to examine it. Turned it over and bent down to look closely at some printing on the inside. She read it aloud, “Everything Plastic, Keene, New Hampshire.” With a shout of joy, she pulled out her cell and googled what appeared to be a company name. “My gosh,” she exclaimed. There was a website for the company—in Keene, New Hampshire. Appeared to still be in business making plastic toys and other things. She dialed the number, her finger shaking with excitement.

“Everything Plastic,” said the man who answered. “This is Frank. What can I do for you?”

She had to calm herself down. Took a deep breath before responding.

“Hello, this is Kathryn Mackie, calling from Boston—the Gardner Museum in Boston. I’ve been going through some old inventory, and I came across some plastic souvenirs that I think you made for us years ago.”

“Yeah, that could be so. We’ve been around for a while. You need some more?”

“Well, not exactly. First, I guess, is whether you’d still have anything to do with these items today—it’s been forty or fifty years since you made them.”

“You say The Gardner Museum. Didn’t I just see a Netflix movie about the old robbery at that museum—years ago? This have anything to do with that?”

Thinking, quickly, *Couldn't have this guy tying this to the theft.*

"No, no. Nothing to do with that. We have . . . have a bunch of artist workshops here at the museum. They work in clay, and pottery, and different mediums. One of the students has evidently become enamored with this souvenir—it's actually an eagle—a bronze eagle—and she wants to try to make it in clay. Her teacher's a friend of mine and I offered to try to find out whether you might still have the original mold, or whatever you used to make it."

"You say forty or fifty years ago? What about more recent purchases?"

"I don't think so. We still have a bunch of them. Doesn't look like they sold very well."

"I guess I can look. By the way, I'm Frank Hardy. My father would have been running the place back then. We never throw away anything, you know. A New Hampshire thing. Probably going to take a while, though. Your name was?"

"Kathryn Mackie." *Wouldn't tell him her position.* I'm on the staff here. I'll give you my number, and we'll gladly pay for your efforts and purchase anything you find."

"Yeah, okay. A bronze eagle, you say? And how big?"

"About ten inches high, with spread wings. It was actually for the top of a flagpole—so, hollow in the middle—they call it a finial."

"I got it. All written down. I'll see what I can find. Call you back."

"The student is going to be very excited that I was able to track you down, Mr. Hardy. This'll make her day."

"Let's not get carried away, Ma'am. I said I'd look. Don't know if I'll find anything."

"Sure. I understand. We really appreciate this."

Chapter Nineteen

More Phone Calls

After talking to Frank Hardy, Kate wanted to yell for joy, but settled for pumping her fist with a satisfied grin. If this guy could find the mold they used to make the plastic copy, she could use it to make a golden duplicate. As Jonathon would be sure to point out, there were a couple of ifs there. But now on a roll, she decided to continue and try to reach her old boss, Bill McLaughlin. She still had his number. Maybe he did still have the hots for her. She hoped so.

"Secret Service. How can I help you?"

"I'd like to speak with Chief Bill McLaughlin."

"Yes, and is he expecting this call, Ma'am?"

"Not exactly. This is Kathryn Mackie. I used to work for him—in the protective service. I think he'll be willing to talk with me. It's pretty important."

"Mr. McLaughlin is not available now, Ma'am, but I'll forward your message. Is there a number you'd like to leave?"

"Yeah, sure. Here's my number—thanks for the help."

So now she had to wait for two call backs, either of which could make or break her grand scheme. She figured, *Might as well make the third call to Florida.* Sooner or later, she had to talk again with Professor Henry David Conan. He was really the key to this whole thing, since, after all, he was the original alchemist. His mother had named him after Henry David Thoreau of Walden Pond, expecting him to grow to a man of great ability. She had not been disappointed. He had spent years studying the art and science of alchemy until he finally met with success.

Two years ago, Conan had his right thumb sliced off while being questioned by a Cuban squad trying to steal his secret processes for making gold. Mackie's boss, Perkins, then pretty much held his severed thumb as hostage to make the professor cooperate with the CIA. Once he agreed to help, they reattached his thumb. Conduct like that had turned her against government service and led her to quit and go into the private sector. She punched in his 239 exchange number in Florida.

"Hello, Agent Mackie? Is this really you? Didn't expect to hear from you again. Thought we were finished after we made those coins."

"So did I, Professor. So, did I. But I've become involved with something in my new job in Boston. I'm now running security at the Isabella Stewart Gardner Museum in Boston. . . ." "No way," he exclaimed. "I was almost across the street when I worked at Boston University. I know the museum. A wonderful place."

"I'd forgotten you worked up here before going to Florida Gulf Coast University."

"Yes. It was actually up there where I fit the final piece into the puzzle. Where I found Newton's journal and learned about the importance of the sun's heat."

"Okay, well, the reason for my call, Professor. We have one more small job to do . . ."

"Not making more gold?" he said. "You promised we were finished. And the government told us we were finished. I've put all that behind me."

"Look, Professor. I know what I promised, and what you've been through. But this is real important. It'll be a one-time pour. And I'm pretty sure the government's going to give us their okay."

"And the Israelis? And the Cubans? Are they going to give us an okay?"

"They won't even know about it, Professor." *She hoped that was right.*

"Henry," *getting personal,* "this is still very preliminary. Just sort of a heads-up call. Just wanted to make sure you were still there and still able to help. What I want to do is fly down there in the next week or so and go over everything with you. We'll only do this if you're comfortable. No one's going to force you to do anything. You're still there, right next to the river, with all your systems running?"

"I'm still next to the river, but you've probably heard about our hurricane. Did some damage here. It'll have to be repaired."

"We can go over that when I get there. I'll call first. And, Professor, as before, not a word about this to anyone."

"Kate, what are you getting me into?" She was off the line.

A few minutes later, McLaughlin called back.

"Kathryn Mackie, just can't get rid of you, can I?" He laughed, "What's so important now, Kate?"

"First, I should probably thank you for your recommendation to the Gardner Museum. I landed the job."

"Yeah, I heard that you were now protecting art, rather than people."

"It's that art I'm calling about, Bill. You've probably heard about the big art robbery up here years ago."

"Sure. I think everyone's heard about the Gardner heist."

"I'm working on that, Bill. Might have come up with a way to recover the stuff. But I need some help—probably from the FBI."

"And you call good old Bill McLaughlin to help with the FBI?"

"Sort of, Bill. What I need is some entrée from you to the new AG—John Fenton. The FBI works for him."

"Yeah, isn't he the guy you called an asshole when you were down here a month ago?"

"I did get a little carried away. I'm hoping he doesn't carry a grudge—he also gave me a pretty good recommendation up here. This could be a real coup for the FBI. They could help solve the biggest unsolved robbery there is. All I need is a chance to talk to him and explain the situation. He might tell me to pound sand. But he might want to get a huge win for his agency."

"And I guess you're not going to tell me any more about this big plan of yours?"

"Really gotta hold this pretty close to the vest, Bill. All I'm asking is fifteen minutes of his time."

"Hey, look. I do talk to him pretty regularly. I'll tell him you called; want a short meeting. Can I also tell him you apologize for calling him an asshole?"

"Definitely, Bill. I am sorry about that."

Then she got the other call back. From New Hampshire.

"You're in luck, Miss Mackie," Frank Hardy announced. "I found the account, with all the paper-work and a slightly dusty ten-inch-tall eagle mold."

"That's great, Mr. Hardy. The student will be so pleased. Now, can we get it from you—we'll pay of course."

"No need to pay. It's not worth much to us. But you could do me a favor in return. Get me on your shop's approved vendor list and put in a good word for us. Looks like we haven't done any work for the museum in many years. We still make great souvenirs. Replicas of museum art. Stuff like that."

"No problem. I can definitely do that, Frank. Now, let me give you our address."

"Oh, I have the address, Miss Mackie. Went on to your website. And I see you're head of security. And that eagle appears to be one of the items taken in that robbery. So, I have the address." He laughed, "Don't worry. Doesn't really matter to me why you need the mold. Not doing us any good up here."

"Thank you very much, Mr. Hardy. I hope I'll someday be able to show you what our . . . student can do with it."

He's a perceptive bastard, isn't he?

Then she heard back from the secret service chief.

"You're in luck, Kate. Fenton's going to be in Boston next week at a judicial conference. He'll try to fit you into his schedule—either with him or his assistants. Says it better be good."

"It's good, Bill."

"Okay, he has your contact information. His office will be in touch with you. And, Kate, you owe me."

Her last call was from a blocked number.

"This is Kathryn Mackie."

"Kate. John Perkins. Need to talk to you."

"Hello to you, also, John. Thought our business was over long ago, so what do we have to talk about?"

"It should have been over, Kate, but I'm told you're telling stories and naming names."

"Look, John, I was dragged down to Washington and almost accused of being a traitor. I told the truth about what happened with your little task force. Nothing but the truth. I understand the Vice President has denied that our final meeting ever took place. Who knows? Maybe he has memory issues. I was told the matter is closed, and it certainly is in my mind. So that's about all I have to say."

"Just remember who you're dealing with, Kate. I think you know I protected you from being hurt in Florida. But I'm not the one calling the shots now. This is just a heads up. I wish you great success in your new career, but don't fuck with people in high places."

"Message received, John. Loud and clear. You be well," disconnecting the call.

Chapter Twenty

The Attorney General Meeting

Monday morning the following week, she heard from the Attorney General's office. One of his assistants called—sounded like the Chet she had met before.

"Miss Mackie, this is one of the Attorney General's assistants."

"Yes, Chet isn't it?" *Why didn't they like to give their names? Too important? Or too unimportant?*

"Yes, we and the Attorney General will be in Boston on Wednesday—at the Federal courthouse for a conference. He'll be tied up most of the day, but he's asked us to meet with you about something you think is important to talk about."

At least not a brush off, she thought. "Yes, that's great—really appreciate it. I think you'll be interested in what I have."

"We might be, Ma'am. But we'd like a little heads up before the meeting. Like, tell us what the heck is going on."

"Sure." *No sense holding back now.* "It's about the old art heist at the Gardner Museum over thirty years ago. Some say the biggest robbery in history. It's never been solved and nothing's ever been recovered. I'm now working at the museum. I've spent the last month going over everything about the robbery, and I think I've come up with a way to solve it and get the art back."

"That would be big, Miss Mackie. But why are we involved—The Attorney General's office?

"Cause I'm going to need some law enforcement help. Specifically, the FBI."

"Why not the local police? Boston has a big force—supposed to be pretty good."

"I need the best, Chet. For the biggest theft in history, I need the best. I'll tell you all about it Wednesday. Where should we meet?"

"We'll be at the Courthouse all day. Mostly in the large courtroom on the third floor—think they call it the Moakley room. Come over about two o'clock and we'll look for you outside the courtroom. We'll get a room somewhere."

"I'll be there, Chet."

Mackie reported her progress to museum director Ketchum and that she'd be seeing the Attorney General on Wednesday.

"Remember, Kate, you don't have a green light yet. Let's see what they think about your idea. Let's see if they're willing to help."

She finally learned their full names when they met. Chet was Chet Mooney. The one she called Calculator Man, Michael Broom. They led her to an attorney's conference room, took seats, listened intently and took copious notes as she explained her plan. She soon learned that the shorter man—Broom—was in charge.

"So bottom line," summarized Broom, "is that you think you can make a fake golden eagle, advertise that the thieves have surfaced and you're about to pay them a lot of money, and you think that will draw out the real guys who have this art." Pausing, "That about it?"

"Put that way, Mr. Broom, you make it sound pretty simple. But, yes, that's what I want to do."

"And why, after thirty years, hasn't someone else come up with this idea?" added Chet.

"Don't know, sir. It is a little outside the box—using deception and fakery to draw someone out."

"And you say you can come up with this fake golden eagle which will be good enough to pass expert inspection?"

"I can do that. I've got everything lined up . . ."

"Let's not kid each other, Mackie. We've read your report. You're going to try to make this golden eagle yourself, aren't you?" said Broom.

"Well, as you know, I do know how, and no one's offered us six pounds of gold yet. But not a single person—except whoever has the stuff—is going to be misled or defrauded or hurt in any way. If it doesn't work, we fold our tent and announce it was another fake claim for the reward which we uncovered before paying. That fake eagle can then go wherever you want—Fort Knox as far as I'm concerned. It'll be real gold, but in the overall scheme of things, an insignificant amount. If the operation fails—if the thieves don't come forward—no one will even know the FBI was involved. You'll be heroes if we succeed, but blameless if we fail."

"So, you're not asking us, or the FBI, to get involved in anything other than tracing and apprehending the thieves if they surface, right? We don't even have to know how you make the darn thing—the . . . finial," added the other assistant.

"Correct, sir."

"Okay", said Broom, "we understand." He looked at his partner and they nodded at each other. "I admit we're intrigued by the idea. Could be a huge win for the FBI. Not much downside that I see right now. We'll talk to some folks and get back to you. Oh, one final thing Mackie," Broom added.

"Yes?"

He took off his glasses and stared at her, "As I said, we read the report you gave us in Washington. If this crazy idea today had come from any other source, we'd probably move to get you committed. But we admire your past work—as does the Attorney General—except when you called him an asshole—and, for that reason, we'll give it some serious consideration."

"That's all I ask. Thank you, sir."

"The Attorney General has also told us to advise you that you'll soon be hearing that the Vice President is withdrawing from the presidential race to pursue other interests once his term ends. It's being blamed on this crazy idea he's pushed to make Israel our fifty-first state. No other reason. We'd just as soon you not think or suggest that there's any other reason."

"I understand, sir. I'm completely on board. Thanks again for considering my idea."

Chapter Twenty-One

Planning for Florida

The next day the eagle mold was delivered. Carefully packaged in bubble wrap, Mackie found there were actually two molds. One for the front of the bird and one for the back. They looked like they were ceramic—chalky white and unimpressive. Sort of the reverse image of what would be the final product. She shrugged while repackaging them. Hoped the professor would know what to do with them. She called him.

"Hello, Kate. Been waiting for your call. You caught me by surprise last call—I was nervous—still am—but I'm on board. As long as the government has no objection, I'll try to help. I've even started to get some of the hurricane damage repaired. I lost two of the parabolic mirrors—the posts were blown down and one mirror shattered. But the other appears to be intact, so I'm having the post set up again and everything rewired. I think three mirrors will give us enough solar heat. And my water channel from the river was flooded and contaminated. I'm trying to get it cleaned out by a guy without using any machines . . . you know, machinery would probably contaminate it. Everything has to be natural for the process to work."

"Whoa, slow down, Professor. Let me get down there and go over what we're going to need. It's great you're jumping right in, but I need to go over everything with you."

"Is it still on, Kate? I'm spending some money down here."

"It's definitely still on. You just surprised me with everything you're already doing. Don't worry about the costs. I'm going to cover everything. I'm looking at next week—probably get there Monday night. Any chance of staying at your place so we can work full time on this?"

"Plenty of room, Kate." He paused, "I'm starting to get excited—and curious. This was my life, you know."

"I know, Henry. I know all too well. So, I'll see you Monday evening—I can get there on my own from the airport. Oh, by the way, how's the thumb?"

"I guess okay. They did a pretty good job reattaching it. Just not much movement. But almost no one notices it. In any event, I'm just going to assist you. It's going to be your hands that do the work, Kate. As you know, I lost the power when the girl died."

"No violence this time, Henry. I promise. A few days and we'll be done and I'll be out of your hair before anyone even knows I was there."

Mackie had reported her meeting with the AG's assistants to both Jonathon and Ketchum. She told both she was going to Florida to see if she could make the golden eagle.

"I've done it before, on a smaller scale, so I need to show this mold to Professor Conan and figure out whether we can pull it off. I'm pretty sure the FBI's going to be on board. I'd like to be ready to move once they are."

Jonathon was supportive. Ketchum, less so.

"Kate, I'm still very nervous about the entire idea. And I don't see how I can authorize it without board approval. For you, it's just a new job. For me, my job and reputation's on the line here." Mackie knew she was going to lose the opportunity unless she came up with some wiggle room.

"Ma'am, how about this. How about you go to the executive committee while I'm away—not the full board—and explain my proposal to them. Then, when I return from Florida, if I've been successful, I'll sit down with them and go over everything. If I can't convince them, we don't go forward." *But, when I plop a foot-high golden eagle finial on the table in front of their eyes, they'll buy in. They'll want to be heroes. To do what no one's been able to do in thirty years.*

"Okay," the director sighed, waving goodbye, "go to Florida. I'll talk to the committee. Have a safe trip."

Chapter Twenty-Two

In Florida

Her Uber ride drove her up the long driveway to Conan's one-story ranch house Monday evening. The only glitch had been at airport security in Boston, and then the flight attendant wouldn't let her carry on the eagle mold, which was carefully packed in her carry on bag. They finally compromised and let her check it at the plane's door, to be returned outside the door when they landed. *Gee,* she thought, *what are they going to do on the way back if I'm carrying a six-pound golden eagle?*

The professor's house was on a large parcel of land just east of Fort Meyers, on the Caloosahatchee river. The area used to be made up of small cattle ranches. It was not far from the university where the professor taught physics. He came out the front door to greet her and help with the bags. He was a short man. She saw that he still wore shoes with a half inch lift.

"It's good to see you again, . . . agent? . . . Miss? . . . Mackie?"

"Let's make it Kate, Professor. I'm no longer an agent, but you're still the professor in my mind, and that's the way I'll always think of you. I'm not being formal. It's just that, in my mind, you'll always be the professor."

In her mind, she also knew he carried a bit of a flame for her. She always politely fended him off—kept a little formality between them.

"Fine with me, Kate."

She put her carry on bag on the table, opened it, and carefully unwrapped the ceramic molds. Then she pulled out an eight by ten photograph of the original golden finial and laid it next to the molds.

"That's what we have to duplicate, Professor. As you used to say when you taught me the process, we have to duplicate that old golden eagle with a new one. Make some new gold that's indistinguishable from old gold. Can we do it?"

Professor Conan picked up the front mold and examined it carefully.

"Looks like it was used to make a plastic replica before."

"Exactly right."

He walked over to his laptop and spent a few moments typing in numbers and queries. "Question is whether the mold will take the heat of molten gold—that's two thousand degrees, you might remember." He finally nodded and looked up. "We can probably do it, but only once, because I think the heat will damage the mold. No second try, Kate."

"That's okay, Professor. I don't plan to do it twice. Now," pausing, "one other change. The new gold has to be eighteen karat—not pure twenty-four karat like we did before."

"That doesn't surprise me," he murmured as he continued to work on his computer. "Twenty-four karat would be too soft for something like this," pointing to the eagle in the photograph. "That means we'll have to add some copper during the melt—a quarter of the weight will have to be copper, mixed with the gold. Perfectly normal for jewelry and decorative items. Holds up a lot better than pure twenty-four karat. And then, we're going to have to join the two halves together. I think there's a gold-like solder we can use to do that."

"How do you remember all this stuff, professor? Perkins stole all your notes."

"Yes, he did, but, as you probably remember, they won't be any use to him because of the error factor I added to all the numbers. Since gold's atomic weight is slightly over 196, I reduced every number in my notes to ninety-six percent of the actual number. They'll never figure that out. And, as we know, a person who doesn't believe and has done evil things, cannot be a successful alchemist. That's how I lost the power when I killed that girl, even though I had some justification. Perkins and his CIA crowd are certainly worse than me. They could never make gold, even with accurate numbers.

"I've now managed to reconstruct everything from memory, with quite a bit trial and error. Remember, it's a one to nine ratio. I need one part old gold added to nine parts lead. They're exposed to the right amount of moonlight for the right length of time. Then they have to be heated with sunlight to six hundred twenty-one degrees for the lead and nineteen hundred forty-seven degrees for the gold.

"Because the metals are so close in atomic weight, the lead atoms are then attracted to the gold atoms—almost like magnetism—and the combination becomes ten parts gold. And because of the different atomic weights, the resulting new gold weighs very slightly less than old gold. It passes all the tests for gold: nitric acid, electronic conductivity, even weight tests, unless they're taken to tenths of a gram. The weight discrepancy is less then one percent. But as you know, I, and unfortunately the Israelis also, have managed to correct that weight discrepancy by a very slight adjustment of the one to nine ratio."

"I'm glad you're here to understand all that, Professor. But what about the weather? Is it going to be alright this week?"

"Glad you remembered that, Kate. We'll need a nice full moon, followed by a day of bright sunshine. The sunshine will be real important, since I have only three working mirrors. Got to get it to that critical two thousand degrees. I've checked, and Wednesday night will be a great moon, with full sun on Thursday. We need both, to first fertilize the metals with moonlight, then to transform them with sunlight. So, we should plan on Thursday for the pour.

"Tomorrow I'll go shopping for what we'll need. I still have a little old gold for the starter with the lead. We'll need the copper, and the solder, and naturally, the lead. I still have the pouring pots and utensils we used when we made the coins. And, as you know, I've pretty much reconstructed all my notes and calculations which they stole."

"Yeah," she answered. "Pretty sure it was Perkins who took our stuff, cause the Israelis already knew the process. Perkins thought he'd do it himself. Bet he was surprised. He was rotten through and through. As you just said, he could never be an alchemist. Bad people cannot make gold."

The professor stood from his computer, "So that's about it." He looked over at her, "Now, are you going to explain why we're doing all this?"

"Sure, Professor, you're certainly entitled to know the entire story. So let me tell you what's going on in Boston. You have something cold—iced tea or something? We'll go over everything."

"Great. Then I have this good restaurant for dinner. It's just down the highway—a real Boston experience—The Clam Bake. Great New England seafood."

"Guess we have to eat somewhere, Professor."

The meal was good. She had the fried clam plate—he the swordfish. They talked about their jobs.

"I'm brand new at the museum, but I think it's going to be sort of a fun experience running all their electronic security systems, and maybe adding a few new wrinkles. There're a lot of motion detectors and cameras, but when it comes right down to the bottom line, it's the staff on the ground that's most important. They found that out after the big theft. Hopefully, the theft is going to be off my plate if we're successful in this operation. I'll then be able to concentrate on day to day operations. I'm also still seeing the same guy in Washington—we're pretty serious. What about you, Professor? How's the teaching going now that your days with gold are behind you? What's going on in your life?"

"I'm finding I enjoy the new areas of engineering and physics. I'm now focusing on the green stuff—battery storage capabilities; recycling; controlling waste. The students eat it up, and it's less all-consuming than my previous fixation on gold. So maybe you helped me by putting a stop to my making gold. Must admit it's a little less profitable. But I have enough to be fine. And I actually have a little of my "new" gold stashed away for a rainy day. As for my life, not much happening on the personal side."

"Why don't you keep that bit about the new gold to yourself, Professor."

"That's my plan."

Before falling asleep that night, Mackie went over in her mind what Professor Conan had told her about his goldmaking—his alchemy—when she first encountered him. He had spent years as a young scientist reviewing historical treatises on the subject. He became fixated on transforming lead to gold. After many failures, he had uncovered a small journal by the famous Sir Isaac Newton—found it in Boston—which finally gave him the key. He had to use the moon—mother of all matter, and the sun—father of all matter. Using the rays of the Florida sun, he had finally succeeded.

He had explained to her that alchemy was not just a science—it was almost a religion, requiring the alchemist to be pure in mind and heart. He had lost his talent after he killed a woman and became tainted. She was one of the Cubans who had taken his thumb, and although he had acted at least partially in self-defense, he had caused a death—taken a life. So, he lost his ability to be an alchemist. He then taught his skills to Kate Mackie. He could no longer be directly involved. He could assist and advise, but he could no longer make gold with his own hands.

Two years ago, she would have put this all down as nonsense. But she'd seen it work. She had seen his ability disappear and hers take its place. She couldn't explain it, and she would be labeled crazy if she tried, but she had seen with her own eyes that lead could be turned into gold. She had done just that when she sent out the "fake" Israeli coins which had caused her to be summoned to Washington.

Chapter Twenty-Three

Planning to Make Gold

Tuesday was shopping day for the professor. Mackie stayed behind to deal with regular museum business by email. She did have a new job which required her attention. When he returned, he pulled her aside.

"Kate, maybe I'm being paranoid, but I'm sure someone was following me. A gray pickup seemed to be everywhere I was. Never got a clear look at the driver, but it was a guy—only one guy in the truck, I'm pretty sure."

She thought for a moment.

"Don't think any of our folks would be doing that. They more or less know what we're doing—no need to follow us. And if it was the Israelis, you wouldn't have seen them. I'm sure the Cubans were scared away for good. So that leaves our old friend, John Perkins—the

CIA. The son of a bitch is maybe still around. Let me think a minute, Professor . . ."

"Kate, I don't want any more trouble," he said nervously. "You promised, no more trouble."

"I'll keep that promise, Professor. But I have an idea," pointing at him. "Let's you and I take a little road trip. We have some time. Let's drive down to the closed prison in east Naples where Perkins was trying to set up his gold making operation. It'll only take an hour. I want to see if anything's still going on there. Then, depending on what we see, I'm going to send Mr. Perkins a short message which will get him off our backs. We're not going to have trouble from him."

They drove south on Interstate 75, through the toll booths, and then about ten miles into the Everglades. They exited north onto Route 29 and then east on Oil Well Road, where Kate directed Conan to stop at a small convenience store. She went into the store for some information.

"Hello, trying to find the old prison—Hendry Correctional—am I close?"

"You're close, Ma'am, but you're not going to find much there. Closed a few years back. Pretty much deserted, now."

"My brother used to be incarcerated there. Promised him I'd get some pictures proving it's closed to guarantee he'll never go back." She laughed, "Sort of a joke—maybe a little sick—but I promised."

"Six miles down the road, Ma'am. Might be a caretaker or someone living there to keep the riff raff out. But other than that, I think you'll find it empty. You can probably take as many pictures as you like."

They drove the six miles till they saw the tall walls and barbed wire surrounding the complex. It was clearly shuttered and closed, but as they parked by the front gate, they saw one vehicle parked partly behind a building. It was a pickup truck—a gray one.

"That the truck that was following you, Professor?"

"Can't say for sure, but it sure looks like it. Same color."

"Well, you might not have known, Professor, but Perkins rented this place from the state to try to run a CIA-backed gold making facility here. You certainly remember that you and I were here for a short while till we closed it down. I'm sure he's not making gold here but looks like he might be using it as some sort of home base." She twirled her finger to turn around. "Let's get out of here and head back so I can send him my goodbye message. Tell him goodbye, and to get the hell out of our lives."

She sent the following email to the address she thought was probably still good:

John. We know you're here and following us. This is a very small and discrete operation for a private party in Boston. It is fully supported by the FBI. If you don't disappear and leave us alone, my report, which you're aware of, will be released to the media immediately.

Chapter Twenty-Four

The Intruder

On Wednesday, Kate received a response. When she opened the email, it said simply, "Message Received and Complied With." After ten seconds, the message disappeared from her screen in a silent explosion of dots. They then set everything up for the pour to take place the next day.

That night, Kate was sleeping in a guest room in the back of the house, on the river side, when something woke her. She looked at her watch. Two thirty a.m. A quiet purring sound was coming from the river—like a small outboard engine. Then it stopped. Right behind the house. She rolled out of bed and went to explore. No sense waking the professor, she thought. He'd simply panic. But she needed a weapon. She looked around in the darkened house—luckily there was a full moon as they had planned—but saw nothing useable. Then she remembered the hammer—the ballpeen hammer they had bought. It was outside on the porch table with the other tools waiting for the pour. She exited through the front door and walked slowly and quietly around the side to the back.

Sure enough, there was a figure approaching the porch from the river. Barely visible in the moonlight. Kate quietly leaned over the porch rail and grasped the hammer. The figure was wearing some type of goggles and raising something to her eyes—taking pictures. *Night goggles and photographing our set up. Had to be the Israelis.*

Kate approached quietly from behind, getting quite close, before announcing herself.

"What the hell you doing here?"

The figure spun quickly and reached a hand to its back. Mackie's Secret Service training took charge, and she struck her left arm out forcefully with knuckles closed into a wedge, striking the figure in the throat with all her power.

"You bitch," gasped a woman's voice, as her hands went to her throat and she gasped for breath. Without hesitating, Mackie swung the hammer hard with her right arm and struck the woman on the outside of her left knee.

"Goddamnit, you broke my fucking knee," the woman gasped as she sucked for air and fell to the ground.

Not stopping, Kate reached down and pulled a pistol from the holster at the woman's back. A Glock 19. She stepped back, pointing it at the figure on the ground.

"You wanna tell me what the hell you're doing here before I shoot out the other knee?"

As she expected, the woman was silent, moaning quietly and grasping her knee.

"Yeah, Mossad don't talk, do they." She stayed a distance away. "Well, let me do the talking, then. You're going to hobble back down to the river and get in your boat and get the hell out of here."

"I can't walk, bitch. I need some help."

Mackie looked around and spotted a shovel in the dirt pile by the trench to the river.

"Sure, you can, lady. You can crawl over and grab that shovel and use it as a crutch—or a cane—I don't give a shit. Then you get your ass out of here. If you don't make your boat, the alligators will be glad to help drag you to the river. That's what they did with the last woman who was left out here. And, since you're bleeding a bit, they'll find you." She paused, "We understand each other?"

The woman nodded.

"And, tell your boss, if you guys come near us again, I'll have your entire gold operation which is taking place in the desert at Qumran on *60 Minutes* in very short order."

Chapter Twenty-Five

The Pour

The professor hadn't been wakened by the scuffle, and Mackie decided not to tell him about it. It would only scare him, and maybe make him walk away. She had checked the river area an hour after the confrontation. She'd heard the boat's engine start, and when she checked, the boat was gone, as was the shovel.

Thursday morning, they had all of the supplies and equipment assembled and ready. The lead and old gold had been left outside and exposed to the moonlight the night before, right next to where Mackie had fought the Israeli woman. She had done everything in self-defense, certainly hadn't killed the intruder, and hoped that her aggressiveness hadn't disqualified her as an alchemist. She'd soon find out. Conan's kitchen was in the back of the house facing the river. A large sliding window faced the river, with a covered porch outside the window. A butcher block bench stood on the porch. Running from the river to the porch was a small ditch with a clay pipe along its length. River water from the Caloosahatchee flowed through the pipe and through a filtration system to clean it of impurities.

"I'm adjusting the mirrors now," explained the professor, as he worked on his laptop at the kitchen table. "We're going to have maximum solar heat at one thirty, so that's when we'll start the process. As we did with the coins, I'll stay inside while you're out on the porch. Remember, Kate, you have to let the lead and the slivers of old gold reach two thousand degrees, then put in the copper and let it go for another five minutes. I've got six pounds of lead and two of copper. Stir it a little. Then quickly pour the molten gold into each mold to the top edge. They're in wire baskets so you can then immediately lower them into the running water behind the porch to cool them. The tough part's going to be getting the gold out of the molds. I think if you strike them with the ballpeen hammer, the rounded end, the ceramic molds will shatter, and you'll have the golden eagle in two halves." He looked up, "At least that's the plan."

"And the lead and old gold," she answered. "Did it get enough moonlight last night? Was it fertilized?"

"Won't know till we pour it, Kate. Was a full moon." Pausing, "Then the easy part. We solder them together and polish it up and," holding up crossed fingers, "we have your golden eagle. Have to be confident, Kate. As I've told you, there's a fair amount of science involved. But also, some faith."

At 1:30, Kate checked the temperature gauge at the spot on the table where the three solar rays were focused on an asbestos pad.... 1500 degrees Fahrenheit and rising. She slid over the steel container which held the old gold and lead, proportioned as the professor had directed. When the gauge read 2,000 degrees, she put on the insulated gloves and slid the container under the beam. She closed her eyes and prayed. *Don't know any mumbo jumbo words. Just a silent prayer for success.*

She saw it start to bubble, then puddle at the bottom of the container. It slowly turned from gray to yellow, and she dropped in the copper and stirred slowly with a long-handled steel spoon. Everything merged and melted together, settling into a thick soupy liquid. Looking up to the window, she saw the professor gesture to pour. She then grabbed the two handles with her gloved hands and poured the viscous gold liquid into the two molds, filling each to the brim. Then quickly dropped the two baskets into the cold water, one with each hand, and let them sit for the appointed time. Finally, the professor whispered, "pull them out."

She did so and hit each mold with a short tap from the round end of the hammer—not as hard as she had swung it last night—and the molds shattered, leaving each basket with half a golden eagle. Once the metal cooled, Conan joined her on the porch. They soldered the halves together and polished the surface.

It had gone smoothly. By three o'clock they were looking at a ten-inch, golden eagle perched on the table next to all the equipment.

"Look at that, Professor. Take a look at the best-looking eagle in all South Florida." They stood side by side and gazed at the bird; she with a smile of satisfaction, he with tears. He knew it was probably his last time.

They were celebrating with glasses of wine when Mackie's cell phone rang.

"Miss Mackie?"

"Yes, and who is this? Your number's blocked."

"That's how we do it at the FBI, Ma'am. This is Jim Wilcox, special agent in charge of the Boston office. I understand you might need our help?"

"Oh my gosh! Yes we do," she exclaimed. "How much do you know?"

"I know everything, Ma'am. Read all the reports, the files, probably know about as much as you."

"Well, special agent . . . uh, Wilcox, I'm in Florida. I'm coming back tomorrow with a special package—a bird if you will."

"I think I know what you mean, Miss Mackie."

"Can we meet tomorrow—tomorrow afternoon?"

"That's why I'm calling, Ma'am. I've been told to get this done."

"Okay, great; I fly into Logan early afternoon. I did have some problems coming down getting through security with what I was carrying. Might be more of a problem coming back."

"That's easy to fix. I'll have an agent meet you in Fort Meyers at the airport. He'll get you through security. And he'll fly back with you and get you to my office."

"Sounds like you're ready to move on this, Wilcox?"

"We're the FBI, Mackie. We're ready to move."

Chapter Twenty-Six

Back to Boston

FBI Agent Fernandez called Mackie in the morning, and they agreed to meet at the Jet Blue ticket counter at the airport.

"I'll be one of the few guys in a suit and tie," he said.

"And I'll be the black chick pulling a silver carry on. Oh, one new issue. I took a pistol off an intruder Wednesday night."

"What?"

"Don't worry. Got rid of the intruder. But I need to get rid of the pistol."

"Well, uh, okay, bring it to the airport. I'll take care of it, and then maybe you can tell me what the hell's going on."

"Sure, I'll do that, Fernandez. I'll tell you what you need to know."

She packed the eagle into her carry on, making it necessary to leave a few things at the professor's house. Some running shoes, a jacket, and some pants. He offered to ship them back to her. Before she was picked up, she wanted to talk to Conan about payment for his efforts. She also had to tell him about Wednesday night. "Professor, I hope you're going to read about our success in the next week or so. One way or the other, I owe you big time. I also didn't tell you what happened Wednesday night."

"What happened?"

"Had an intruder. She came in off the river. Was taking some pictures. I'm pretty sure she was an Israeli."

"And . . ." He waited, frowning.

"I got rid of her. She won't be back. They're going to leave us, and you, alone."

He shook his head, "Kate Mackie, I don't know whether to love you or hate you."

"Well, I thought it best to keep quiet about it till after we did our business. But," she added, "As I was starting to say, I need to make sure you get paid something."

"It was great to do something more than give lectures on rare elements and nuclear fusion, Kate. If the museum will pay for some of our costs, that's great. But not out of your pocket."

"No, I'm talking about more than that. This eagle is going to have a pretty short life span. In a week or so, it's going to become history—disappear like the real one. I'm going to try to get it back to you. Six pounds of eighteen karat gold has some real value. I really don't want it kept intact to possibly someday reveal what we've done. It should disappear. So, if I can get it back to you, can you take care of that?"

"You mean, make it disappear?"

"That's exactly what I mean, Professor."

"I'll take care of it," grabbing her hand with both of his and then hugging her tightly. "We were a good team, weren't we, Kate."

The trip was uneventful. Fernandez took the pistol to his car, and then got them through security and onto the plane without a hitch, along with her carry on. As they deplaned in Boston, there were two FBI suits—one guy and one woman—waiting for them. Fernandez shook her hand and said he was going right back to Fort Myers. Something about a fishing trip this weekend. She walked with the two new escorts to a waiting car. They offered to take her bag, but she shook her head no. Wasn't about to give it up. She looked forward to meeting Special Agent Wilcox.

Mackie expected to be going downtown, but she soon learned that the FBI Boston headquarters building was now in Chelsea, across the river, in a brand new building. They pulled into the underground garage, and she was whisked up to the top floor, pulling her bag behind her. She was ushered into a big, but not ostentatious, office where a group of agents stood in a group talking. One, the only black man, stepped out of the crowd and walked to her, extending his hand.

"I'm special agent Jim Wilcox, Miss Mackie. Glad you got here so quickly." Pointing to the others—she saw four more—"This is our team. For now, anyway. It'll probably get bigger. They know who you are. We'll do introductions later." Then, pointing at her case, "Is that the bird? The famous golden eagle?"

"Sure is, sir. Just hatched yesterday."

"Let's see it," he said. "This is the part I find difficult to buy. That you made this thing out of other metals. But I've read the reports, and you have an impressive background, so I guess I'm just going to have to swallow hard and accept that you can make gold. . . . And then maybe introduce you to my wife who will want to be your best friend."

"Didn't think FBI agents were supposed to make jokes, Wilcox," she said with a smile.

"They allow us one a day, Mackie, and that's my one. So, let's get down to business. Let's take a look at this bird."

She opened her case and pulled out a bubble-wrapped object. Looked around for a table, unwrapped it, and placed it in the middle of the table. She could see the eyes of the agents open wide. No one said a word as they moved closer to the table.

"There he is, agent. Or she. Don't know how to tell the difference."

"Pretty impressive, Mackie. Pretty impressive. Can I touch it?"

"Sure. It's not fragile. Don't be surprised by its weight, though. It's about six pounds."

He picked it up and passed it around to his assistants. "You know we're going to have to test it—maybe over the weekend?"

"Probably best if you just keep it for now, sir. Test away. I'd rather not have it in my possession till it's supposed to be delivered to me by the robbers."

"Okay, Mackie, that brings us to this scam we're going to orchestrate. To draw out the robbers. Let's go over that."

"I need your help on one thing first, sir. We've got this all planned out—or sort of—but I haven't got the full go ahead from the museum . . ."

His eyebrows went up, and he frowned . . . she quickly added, "I'm confident we'll get the go ahead—probably Monday. The director gave me authority to go forward with the planning, but she's nervous about the optics of the museum putting out some not fully truthful statements and participating in a scam. She's gone over it with the executive committee—not the full board—and I'm supposed to meet with them Monday morning. I need you there to help convince them. Maybe put on a bit of a dog and pony show?"

"This is a little bit of a surprise, but probably not a game stopper." He looked at his team, "Guys, can we put on a little dog and pony show to get these Boston Brahmins to give us the green light?"

They all nodded and gestured in the affirmative.

"So now, let's go over some of the details of this scam, as Mackie so nicely describes it. Then we'll send Mackie—can I call you Kathryn, or Kate?—home."

"Kate's fine, sir."

"I'm Jim," he replied.

When she got home she called Jonathon.

"I'm home, Jon. And the eagle has landed at the FBI where it's being tested over the weekend. Big meeting Monday morning at the museum to get the final go-ahead. At least, I hope to get the go-ahead. I'm a little nervous about these all too proper museum people. The FBI's going to be there, and they seem really interested in doing this. Even asked me to confirm that the Boston police are not involved. Don't seem to want to share the spotlight. Maybe don't trust them."

"They want the glory, Kate. And they need it, after all the shit the FBI's been through the last few years. They certainly don't want to share it with the police. The glory, I mean."

"Yeah, I guess so. I'll go over to the museum tomorrow—I've been out all week. Make sure my office and the cage are still intact. Hey, guess who I'm sharing it with next week."

"I give up."

"Two FBI agents, Jon. They're putting two in my office, two next to my apartment, and some others spread around. They'll also be on all the phones. They're really all over this. It's starting to get exciting—like the good old days."

Chapter Twenty-Seven

Monday's Executive Committee Meeting

Four heads turned toward her as she entered the museum's Trustee's Room at the appointed ten o'clock. She nodded to director Ketchum, and although the other three were new to her, she had looked them up over the weekend. Chair of the Trustees and of the Executive Committee was Professor Edgar Beale. Probably a direct descendant from the Mayflower. A retired professor from Harvard Law—The Law School—as it was known to its graduates. He was closer to ninety than eighty and looked it. Although seated, he was clearly not a tall man, a bit withered and shrunken with age. The other two faces were women: one the retired head of a local charity, the other the widow of a wealthy benefactor. *At least she was in the majority,*

Mackie thought. But only in gender—they were all very much white. Ketchum made the introductions.

"Kate, this is our chair, Professor Edgar Beale," who stood and raised his hand in hello, "and Marjorie Whitam and Irene Ipswitch, our Executive Committee. The women remained seated but smiled. "Folks, Kathryn Mackie, our new chief of security."

"Thank you for meeting with me," Kate started . . .

"Well, young lady, I think we were the ones who called the meeting." *That's a good start.* "Certainly, sir, I'm here to explain what I'm proposing."

"I think we know what you're proposing, Miss Mackie. Director Ketchum has given us a full report. Looks like you've been a busy girl in your first thirty days. Maybe if you'd been here thirty years ago, you could have prevented this debacle in the first place. But you weren't. And, by the way, I was. A terrible time," shaking his head. "We have to make sure we don't now make it worse with this plan of yours." *Not a good start at all.*

Suddenly, three loud knocks on the door, and in strode Special Agent Wilcox with two agents following, one carrying a large, one-handled black case. Mackie was relieved that at least the two assistants were white. She wasn't sure the professor was current on racial parity.

"This is the FBI, folks," she announced. I told Director Ketchum I would ask them to be here." *And just in time.*

"Good morning. I'm Jim Wilcox, Special Agent in charge of our Boston office, and with me are agents Jonus and Marks." Looking around the room, "If it's okay with you, I have two more agents outside to secure the room, so no one can enter or listen while we talk—or see what we have to show you"—pointing at the box being held by agent Marks.

Beale shrugged and raised his hands, "Whatever you think is necessary, sir."

Jonus went to the door, opened it, and gave a sign to someone outside. Turning, "We're secure, sir."

"The FBI is here to report that we fully support the plan which Miss Mackie has proposed. We've vetted it—all the way to the top—and we think there's a good chance it will reach the people who are holding your art, bring them out into the open, and get the art back where it belongs—here in your museum, into those empty frames. Sir, I think you must be Professor Beale?" looking over at the old man.

"Yes, that's me," he responded holding his head a bit higher.

"Well, Professor, over the weekend I talked with the Director—John Donovan—and you probably don't remember, but he was in your constitutional law class thirty years ago. Actually, right about when this robbery occurred. He remembers the course and asks me to tell you that he still carries the small booklet of our constitution that you passed out in class. He said to give you his best regards and that he hopes you will approve Mackie's plan. We all at the Bureau think it's the best, and maybe only, way to recover your art."

The chill in the air seemed to be melting, and Professor Beale, much more graciously than he had before, spoke again. "Why don't you proceed with what you have, special agent."

"First, what we have here," pointing at the box, "is an amazing replication of your stolen eagle, which Miss Mackie has made, using some special talents that even we don't understand." He pointed at Marks and swung his finger up. Marks placed the box gently on the table, pulled up two side latches, and pulled off the top. Sitting staring at them all was the golden eagle. There were gasps from the trustees.

Wilcox continued, "We first received this from Miss Mackie on Friday. Over the weekend, we've had it fully tested in our labs, and we pulled an independent metallurgist across the river from MIT—sorry Professor," looking over at the old man, "they're probably better known for metals." The professor nodded.

"The results are conclusive. It's fully pure 18 karat gold, same as your original. Then, with the help of Director Ketchum," pointing in her direction, "we located one of your long-term employees who still works here. Joe Mullen does janitorial work, and after being sworn to secrecy—and I mean he was really sworn and so scared to death that I'm sure he'll keep the secret—we had him look at the eagle. He says it looks just like the one he used to dust off regularly in the Short Gallery. So, in conclusion, we have here a golden eagle which is an exact replica of the eagle finial which was stolen from your museum thirty years ago. No one will question that."

"If we put this out right, we think it'll draw out whoever is holding your art. And if we can draw them out, the FBI will find them, apprehend them, and recover your art." He paused, caught his breath, and scanned the room, looking at each one. "That's about it, folks. We need your approval to proceed."

"Very impressive, special agent. Very impressive," said Professor Beale, pausing before continuing. "Our concern has been that we're going to lie to the public when we hold this out as the real thing. It's the museum's reputation that's at stake here."

Mackie knew when to stay quiet. She looked pointedly at Wilcox. He got the hint.

"Beg to differ, Professor," he responded. "We're lying to the thieves—not to the public. The FBI and all law enforcement agencies do this every day. That's how we get undercover agents into criminal enterprises. How we catch financial fraud. How we stop drug deals. Today, we're putting this eagle out as our newest undercover agent. We're gonna fake his pedigree a bit. But it's not going to hurt the public a bit."

Ketchum finally spoke up. "And if this doesn't 'draw them out,' as you say?"

Mackie had thought of this so she spoke out.

"We do just what you did a few years ago when someone tried to collect the ransom by claiming he had the art. A guy named Desper, I think—back in 2017. You figured out he was a fraud and never paid him a cent. Likewise, we won't be paying a cent of ransom unless or until we see and have control of the art."

"And what about the reward, Kate?" Ketchum continued. "Are we going to pay these folks the reward if they return our art?"

"Let me jump in on that one, Director, if you will," Wilcox said. "We clearly have to advertise that the reward, and maybe even more, will be paid to bring these guys out into the open. Even if they stole it in the first place, the statute of limitations on robbery has long run out. I doubt that these guys are the same ones who stole it. Rather, they got hold of the art in some way, and, for some reason, have been sitting on it. Have no idea why. So, yes, you'll probably have to pay at least some ransom to someone. But not before the art is returned."

The professor had been talking quietly and privately with his two committee members. He raised his hand to question, "If we give you the green light, what happens next and what's the time frame?"

Wilcox responded, "Next, on Wednesday, an anonymous delivery to Kate, here at the museum, of a box with the eagle. There'll be a note inside saying the delivery is to prove that the sender has the rest of the art—sort of like what we call proof of life, in a kidnapping. It'll say the remaining art will be delivered upon proper payment. Then, simply, 'We'll be in contact.' Kate will be suitably surprised, amazed, and excited. Probably run screaming to the director." Looking over at her, "Okay, Kate, I see your eyebrows going up. Maybe you won't scream. But you'll be real excited and surprised. You explain the next step, Kate."

She jumped in. "At the recommendation of the FBI, we hold a press conference on Friday. Here at the museum. Probably in Calderwood Hall. We announce the receipt of the eagle, put it on display, and urge the people to contact us to work out details of the exchange. We make it clear we're prepared to pay the ransom, which remains at ten million dollars."

"Why move so fast?" asked Professor Beale.

Wilcox responded, "Thanksgiving's a few weeks away, and then the holidays. We need this done by then. Friday's important. This will be a big story—a really big story—in Boston and across the country. It will be the talk in every bar and party in Boston over the weekend. The Bruins play this weekend—the Patriots in Foxboro on Sunday. I'm sure those announcers will all talk about the story. Remember, we could be dealing with guys who don't watch the news or read the Globe. But they go to bars, and they sure as heck watch the Bruins and the Patriots. By the end of the weekend—probably sooner—these people who have the art are going to hear that we're about to pay someone else. They will be, excuse my French, absolutely bullshit, because they'll know we're dealing with the wrong people. They'll think some imposter is ripping them off. And if we pay someone else, they'll think they've lost their chance to get paid for the real art. We think they'll come forward before the end of the weekend." He paused, caught his breath, and continued.

"We'll have agents in place here at the museum and at Mackie's apartment. We're set to monitor the phones, and we have the ability to trace any incoming calls. We'll be ready to move whenever someone is contacted. It'll probably be Mackie, because you'll put her out during the press conference as the point person. Her phone number will be advertised."

"That's the plan," scanning the people at the table, "and remember, even though I've done most of the talking here, this is Kate Mackie's plan. There's some genius to it. Wish I could say the FBI came up with it, but we're just here to implement it. After all, the FBI doesn't know how to make a golden eagle," pointing to the bird still perched on the table.

"We need your decision, sir," looking straight at the Professor.

"You have it," responded the old man, now sitting straighter than before and with a stronger voice. "Go get the bastards who stole our art and get it back. We're behind you and Miss Mackie one hundred percent."

"We will, sir. But before leaving, one last point. This cannot go beyond this room. Not to spouses, friends, museum workers, anyone. No one beyond those in this room can know what we're really doing. If it gets out, it'll be in the media and on social networks immediately. If that happens, it will fail."

Kate escorted the FBI team out. As they walked down the hall, "You saved the day, Jim," she whispered to him. "Before you walked in, they were about to cancel the whole thing. How'd you find out about the Director being in his class?"

"Well, he did go to the Law School. Not sure exactly what classes he took." He smiled, "Hope the professor doesn't check his class lists."

"And that constitution handout thing?"

"All the professors gave them out," he laughed. "See, I was there, too. A few years later, but I thought he'd be more impressed with our director than a mere special agent, and a black one at that. After all, he already had doubts about one person of color in the room."

Chapter Twenty-Eight

The Eagle Lands

Mackie was in her upstairs regular office Wednesday morning when she got a call from the front desk.

"Miss Mackie, I have a package which was just left for you at the front desk."

"Oh, okay. Who's it from?"

"Don't really know. Some guy came in and left it, saying it was for Security Chief Mackie. Your name's on the box, but no real label. Not real big, but it's pretty heavy."

"Could you have someone bring it up?"

"Sure. Will do."

A young museum volunteer soon knocked on her door jamb. She carried a small box wrapped in brown shipping paper.

"Where should I put this, Ma'am?"

"Just on the floor is fine," pointing to the left of her desk. "Wonder what it is? Doesn't look like flowers."

"Nope. Definitely too heavy for flowers," the girl said as she walked out.

Kate lifted the package to her desk and tore open the wrapping paper. Inside was the same black carry case the FBI had used on Monday. Flipping up the levers, she lifted off the cover and saw her eagle, with the promised note taped to it.

"Guess it's Showtime," she whispered to herself. Took a deep breath and yelled,

"My God, look at this!" She ran into the hall, "Get Ketchum in here! Everyone, come see what was just delivered! I . . . I just can't believe it. I think it's one of the things they stole from the museum. Get some security up here. Don't anyone touch it—might have fingerprints—I'll call the FBI. Oh my god, maybe the stuff's coming back!"

She and Ketchum played their roles perfectly, and before long two FBI agents showed up and took charge. The boxed eagle was carefully removed by the agents for examination, after which the two ladies went into Ketchum's office to make phone calls. More agents appeared and joined them. They remained closeted for a few hours with the FBI, and then they called the museum's head of media relations to join them.

"We need to set up a press conference for Friday morning, Jane," said the director. "Here at the museum—in Calderwood Hall—probably for ten o'clock in the morning." She held up a hand to the young lady adding, "You've no doubt heard that we had one of the old stolen items delivered here this morning. The FBI here—pointing at the two men in the room—want us to hold a press conference to try to reach the robbers to get back the rest of the art. We want both television and print—as much as you can get. Don't give out any details. Just that the museum has some very important news to disclose to the public. Set it up in Calderwood, with a small podium at one end of the room and the press grouped around the floor area. Won't need to use the balconies. And a small table next to the podium." She looked down at her desk and then back up, "Can you handle all that, Jane? It's very important. Put everything else aside."

"Yes, Ma'am. I'll get it done. But I'm not to mention the stolen art, right?"

"Well, you can tease them a bit if you want, Jane. I would say we have an important announcement about a large addition to our collection. But nothing specific. We'll have plenty of information for them on Friday."

Chapter Twenty-Nine

Aiden's Bank Visit

While Mackie had been working diligently on her plan, almost a month had passed since ex-FBI agent Moran had made his last visit to Aiden at the gallery. After the visit, Sean finally gave in to temptation and opened the envelope. He stayed late one evening, locked the gallery door, and opened his safe. The white envelope was now brittle and almost opened itself when he pulled it out of the very back where he had taped it. The envelope still showed the handwritten note—Whiteys Legacy—scrawled sloppily on its face. He peeled it open slowly—he was going to reseal it—and saw a smaller brown envelope. Pulling that out, he saw it contained a key. A small, silver key with some engraved markings. He was perplexed.

"What's it to?" he muttered to himself. There was no explanation of the key or what it could open. He then replaced the larger envelope in his safe, but he kept the smaller one holding the key. The next day, Aiden took the key to a locksmith shop he found online in Quincy, a few miles south of Southie. He didn't want to be recognized making this visit in South Boston.

"Yes, sir, what can I do for you?" he was greeted as he entered the small shop. He had waited on the sidewalk till he was pretty sure no customers were inside.

"I hope so. Have a key here I found cleaning out my Dad's stuff—he passed a few weeks ago. I can't figure out what it's for. Should I just throw it out?" He handed the key to the man behind the counter who pulled it up to his eyes, then reached for a magnifying glass to look closer.

"It's definitely a key for a bank safe deposit box," he said under his breath. "Usually, they have a bank number imprinted somewhere telling you which bank," continuing to examine it—even the edges.

"There it is. I see the number. Now all I have to do is find this little book I have somewhere which will tell us the bank that number applies to." He turned and started to shuffle papers on a shelf behind him. "There it is. Opening a small booklet and running down lists of numbers with his finger. "Bingo! Hey, you got a good one. Bank of Boston—now I think Bank of America. The box number's on the key. Box 100 at the bank." He looked up at Aiden, "Hey, you might have something here. Maybe your old man left you something in the box—maybe you got something valuable. Sounds like a pretty important box—number a hundred and everything. You can call the bank and find out where it is."

"I'll do that," Aiden answered, taking back the key, and turning to leave. "Thanks very much for your help. Can I pay you something?"

"Nah, it was nothing. But maybe let me know what you find—split the millions with me," he laughed. What'd you say your name was?"

"Kevin MacDonald," Aiden answered quickly as he left the shop.

He called Bank of America and was routed to a number of different people before reaching someone who seemed to know about the bank's safe deposit boxes.

"An old key, you say, to Bank of Boston—box one hundred?"

"Yeah, that's what it says, and my locksmith tells me it's a Bank of Boston key."

The lady paused a few moments, evidently looking at some records, then saying,

"Well, sir, what I can say, is that it's probably at 100 Federal Street, downtown Boston. Originally the Bank of Boston building—you know, the one known as the pregnant building—cause it bulges out. Now it's Bank of America. For anything more, you'll have to take your key down there, with proper identification, and see what they have."

"What do you mean, proper identification?"

"Sir, you can't get into a safe deposit box with just the key. What if you found it on the street? Or stole it? No, you need to be the person who set the box up. Need to have the identification to prove that. Sometimes, usually after a death, people have to go into court and get some type of court order saying they can open the box. So that's about all I can do for you, sir. What did you say your name was?"

"Oh, Kevin . . . Kevin MacDonald. Yes, thank you. You've been very helpful."

He'd gone this far. No sense stopping now. Either he'd get into the box or they'd send him home. So next morning he visited the bank and was directed to a below ground level area—the vault—where the safe deposit boxes were located.

"Good morning, sir. You want to access your box?"

"Yes. Here's my key."

"My goodness," the lady said when she saw the key. "That's an old one. And for box one hundred. That's a big one. Let me check our records here." Looking at some records, "Oh, my gosh, the box hasn't been opened in almost thirty years! Are you, are you Sean Aiden?"

He just stood staring at her, unable to think or say anything.

"Sir, are you okay?"

"Ye . . . Yes, I'm okay. And, yes, I'm Sean Aiden. Here . . . here's some id—whatever you need," handing her his license and a few other cards.

"Where have you been, Mr. Aiden? Where have you been for all these years?"

"I've been away. Just want to check what's in the box."

"That's your right, sir. You've got the key, and it's your name on the account. So, let's go in and find box one hundred."

They found it. She inserted Aiden's key, along with another she carried, and then turned to leave, saying,

"I'll leave you to look in your box. Take whatever you want. It's yours. Just ring that buzzer"—pointing at a button on the wall—"when you're finished. I'll come back in and lock it all back up."

He was alone and shaking like a leaf. Was it full of cash? Diamonds? Maybe even drugs? He started to pull the drawer out, lifted the lid, and immediately knew what was there. On top, a rolled and slightly folded over painting, with more rolled and flat canvasses below it. Lying in the very back of the drawer, an eagle. He remembered those pictures of the stolen Gardner art the FBI had given him many years ago. This was it. Whitey's Legacy was the Gardner Museum art.

He reached in and gingerly lifted a few of the canvasses. The one folded on top was the largest—Rembrandt's *Lady and Gentleman*. Then rolled under it was another Rembrandt—*Christ in the Storm*. And *The Concert*. More below lay flat.

He decided to get the hell out of the room before someone else saw it. He wanted nothing to do with it. He wasn't a thief. Why did Whitey set him up like this? He started to push the drawer shut and noticed a small two-inch square etching on top in the front of the drawer. He wasn't ever coming back, but what if someday he had to prove what was in the drawer? Would that ever happen? He didn't know, but almost without thinking he grabbed the small etching and put it in his pocket, slammed the drawer shut, and pushed the button. He was almost running for the exit when the lady banker returned.

"Wait, Mr. Aiden. Your key. You have to take your key," pulling it out and handing it to him.

"Yes, thank you. I'm in a hurry now. Have to run."

Two weeks after his visit to the bank, on the Thursday evening before the Gardner Museum press conference, Sean Aiden received a phone call at his home. He hadn't told anyone—not even his wife, Rosemary—about his discovery at the bank. The envelope was resealed and back in his safe. He couldn't decide what to do. Even if he made an anonymous phone tip, his name was on the box records. They'd soon connect him to the box and arrest him.

"Hello?"

"Yes. Is this Mr. Aiden, Mr. Sean Aiden, owner of the art gallery of the same name?"

He detected the brogue accent—a cultured one—not the Southie roughness.

"Yes. That's me. And who is this, sir?"

"My name is not important, Sean. I need to talk with you about some information we think you possess which concerns Mr. Whitey Bulger."

What the hell is this? "And who are 'we'?"

"Let us just say, we are friends of the late Mr. Bulger."

"As you say, he's dead, and has been so for a while. I know nothing about him or his affairs."

“Our information is a bit different, sir. We are told, and this is from the horse’s mouth, before he died—just before he died—that you hold what’s been referred to as Whitey’s Legacy.

Oh, Jesus, what the hell do they know? “Don’t know what you’re talking about, sir. I repeat, I have nothing of Mr. Bulger’s.”

“I had hoped we could discuss this as reasonable men, Mr. Aiden.”

“We have nothing to discuss, sir,” hanging up. He stood for a moment in silent thought. *Who the hell was that and how much does he know?*

Chapter Thirty

The Press Conference

A podium and a tall pedestal table had been placed at one end of the hall. Calderwood Hall was a forty-foot square, acoustically perfect room in which the museum put on many concerts. It had been created as part of the new addition in 2012. The Hall was surrounded by three levels of glass-fronted balconies, but Mackie and the FBI decided the ground floor alone was all that was needed for the press conference. Jane, the head media associate, had done her job, and soon after nine, Friday morning, the press started to arrive, setting up cameras and microphones facing the podium.

At nine forty-five, two uniformed security officers entered through a paneled door behind the podium and placed a draped shape on the table. They said nothing then took positions on either side of the table, standing at parade rest. Each carried a holstered pistol. They remained silent, ignoring the questions and comments from the press.

"Hey, guys, what's under the drape?"

"Can we take a quick look?"

"Will you shoot us if we try?" To that comment, both officers turned slightly to stare at the speaker, and gave small nods.

At ten o'clock, Marilyn Ketchum and Kathryn Mackie entered through the same door the guards had used. Both were dressed in dark suits, one older and matronly, the second younger and smart looking. Ketchum walked to the podium.

"Thank you for coming on such short notice. I am Marilyn Ketchum, Director of the Isabella Stewart Gardner Museum." Gesturing to Mackie who stood beside her, "This is Kathryn Mackie, our Chief of Security. We have just come from a meeting with the museum's board of trustees. We are here to announce a major triumph for the museum." She looked around the room and stared directly into the cameras. "We announce today that we have opened negotiations with a group to effectuate the return of the art which was stolen from the museum over thirty years ago."

Bedlam broke out, with reporters and newscasters screaming questions and yelling to overshout each other. The two guards stiffened and moved slightly forward. Ketchum held up her hands and pleaded for quiet.

"Please, we will answer all your questions. First," pointing to each of them, "officers, please remove the drape and show everyone what has brought us all here."

Each man turned and seized a corner of the cloth and pulled it gently up and backward, then stepping slightly back and behind the table. At the same time, a spotlight turned on to illuminate the table.

Kathryn's golden eagle stood staring menacingly over his left wing, but from Mackie's point of view, the eagle appeared to be slowly turning its head to size up the whole room.

"This, folks, is the golden eagle which was stolen from us so many years ago. It was recently delivered to the museum as proof that the other art is still intact. It was accompanied by a note saying the people holding our art would soon contact us about the remaining pieces. We're here today to announce to the public that we hope to safely recover all our art and to announce to the persons holding it that we are ready to deal. As you probably know, there is a ten million dollar reward outstanding. We are prepared to pay that reward to the right people." Ketchum paused and took a few moments to compose. "Now, that about does it for me. As our Security Chief, Miss Mackie, here oversees what happens next. Previously with the United States Marshal's Service and the Secret Service, she'll answer your questions and hopefully soon hear from the ones we need to deal with."

Mackie stepped up and took her place at the podium, ready for the first question, which she had planted.

"Miss Mackie," a young reporter yelled, "what's this about a golden eagle? Wasn't it supposed to be bronze, as I remember?"

Mackie pointed at the reporter, "You're right, Ma'am. I wasn't there, but way back at the time of the theft, the FBI wanted the museum to hold some information back to help us test their veracity if any claimants came forward. This was always a golden eagle—pure gold. We said it was bronze to see what any claimant would say. The museum also didn't want to incent someone to simply melt it down for the gold. If bronze, its metal value was pretty small."

"And what about if gold? What's that worth?" Yelled another reporter.

"Let's just say, quite a bit," answered Mackie, "but still far below its historical value." *Now for the real questions.*

"Do you know this is the real thing—the real eagle—and not some inexpensive counterfeit?" asked one of the TV anchors.

"The FBI has run extensive tests in its lab and by independent metal experts. They conclude it's absolutely pure eighteen karat gold. We've also had it examined by Gardner Museum staff who worked on it and cleaned it thirty years ago. They say it looks the same. We're comfortable saying this is our eagle."

"Have you heard again from the thieves?"

"No, we have not. That's why we're here. We want them to know that we have the eagle and we want to talk to them about the rest."

"So, you seem to say you'll pay the ten million reward. What about more?"

Mackie grimaced, "We're not going to negotiate what we're going to pay here on TV. We think ten million dollars is a lot of money and more than enough."

"But you'll pay more, right?"

"Next question, please."

"Is the FBI involved beyond the testing? Are they going to try to catch and prosecute these guys?"

Mackie shook her head. "I'm told there's not much to prosecute. The statute of limitations ran out a long time ago on this robbery. There's a fair chance these folks aren't even the original robbers. In some way, they got possession of our art. The FBI knows what's going on, but right now all we're interested in is paying to get the art back. We're not interested in prosecuting anyone."

Ketchum took her cue and took back the podium.

"That's pretty much everything we have. We do have a handout for you with descriptions of the items stolen and contact information for Miss Mackie. Please feel free to put out her contact information. We want them to call her. Now, you're free to come up for a closer look at the eagle. Please don't touch it."

The two ladies departed, leaving the guards.

Once through the doorway, they walked quickly back to Ketchum's office, where Special Agent Wilcox and his agents were gathered in front of a TV.

"Terrific job!" he exclaimed. "Terrific by both of you. We'll make FBI agents out of you yet," shaking each of their hands. "It's in motion. The plan's rolling. Now, Kate, you sit and wait for the call. Everyone's in place. Your phones are all covered. We just wait."

"So how are you going to trace an incoming call," asked Kate. "Don't you have to have helicopters or planes in the air to triangulate?"

"We used to have to do that," he answered. "But, here in Boston, and in most big cities, we have permanent monitoring pods on the top of some of the tallest buildings. Here I think they're on the Hancock tower, the Millennium, Federal Reserve, and maybe a few others. We turn them on and off as needed. If the call is made within a radius of about twenty miles from the downtown Boston area, we'll be able to trace it. We also have the cell towers."

Chapter Thirty-One

Aiden's Gallery

Friday Morning

Aiden was in his shop at eleven thirty. Since his visit to the bank two weeks ago, all he could think about was what he had seen and what should he do. He would probably be arrested if he reported it. After all, the box had been opened in his name. And his connection to Bulger was evidently well-known. His phone rang.

"Aiden's Gallery," he answered.

"Mr. Aiden, this is your favorite FBI agent—Moran—calling from sunny Florida."

"Yeah," he answered distractedly, "What can I do for you, Moran?"

"Well, Sean, looks like you're off the hook . . ."

"What're you talking about?"

"You watching the news?"

"At eleven thirty in the morning? No, I'm not watching the news."

"It's all over the news, Sean. The Gardner Museum just held a press conference to announce that they're about to get the stolen art back."

"What!" swallowing hard, almost whispering, "Whaddya you mean?"

"They say they've been contacted—some sort of a golden eagle has been returned to them—and they're going to pay ten million, or more, for the rest."

Aiden sat, silent and shocked, saying nothing, staring into space.

"Sean, you still there?"

"Yeah, I'm here."

"This closes the case, Sean. After all these years. And looks like I was wrong about you—unless you sent them that eagle?"

"No, Moran, I didn't send them any goddamned eagle. Now would you please just leave me alone." Hanging up.

He turned on his TV and watched all the reports. He had seen that eagle in the drawer, two weeks ago, with his own eyes. How could it have been delivered to the museum? Absolutely, fucking, impossible. What was going on. He grasped his face in his hands and trembled, tears rolling down his cheeks. What should he do?

Two hours later, Aiden still sat thinking. He knew he should call his wife, but he sat frozen watching the TV.

The front door opened and three men walked in, flipping the Open sign to Closed. The first two looked like typical South Boston thugs—chinos, sweatshirts, big and husky. They weren't young guys. The third looked vaguely familiar. "Billy Bags?" Aiden said with surprise. Hadn't seen the guy in over twenty-five years.

"They don't call me that anymore, Mr. Aiden. Now it's just Billy, or Billy Malloy, which is my real name. I'm retired down on the Cape now. Mr. Bulger got me a good job at the T before he sort of disappeared. They had me doing head counts at the bus stops. I put in my twenty five. I'm retired now. And these two guys are old buddies of Mr. Bulger. They asked me to help them locate someone named Aiden who worked with us back in the day. Obviously, that's you. I guess they want to talk to you. This here is . . ."

"That's okay, Billy," interrupted the larger of the two. You've been real helpful. Why don't you let us talk with Mr. Aiden. The guy outside will drive you back to the Cape. Make sure he gets you that steak dinner we promised," leading him out by the elbow.

Aiden all of a sudden realized this might not be a pleasant visit.

The man returned and stood in front of the art dealer with crossed arms.

"I think someone tried to talk some reason with you last night, Aiden. Right?"

"I got a call, yes."

"And you blew him off, didn't you?"

"Told him I didn't know what he was talking about and couldn't help him, that's right."

"Problem is, Mr. Aiden, we think you're full of shit. We think you know damn well what we're talking about. And we're here to get some answers."

"So why do you think I have something of Mr. Bulger's?"

The man nodded back and forth, raising his arms.

"Maybe a fair question. So, I'll tell you. We think so because Whitey told us so before we killed him."

"But he was killed in prison," Aiden blurted out.

"Yep, that's where he was being interrogated—questioned about where he hid all his loot in Boston before he disappeared. And about who he was about to squeal on. Unfortunately, he didn't last long. But, before his heart gave out, he did say one thing. He said something about Aiden, and a legacy." He shook his head, "That information didn't reach us for a while—not till the guys' lawyers got it back to us—and then it took us a while longer to figure it out. But with the help of Billy Boy who was just here, we think he was telling us that he left some sort of a legacy with you, Mr. Aiden. And now the time for bullshit is over and you're going to tell us just what he gave you."

"I don't know what you're talking about," cried Aiden.

"Okay, have it that way," nodding to his partner. The man turned and waived to someone outside, "bring her in."

Turning back to Aiden, "Look, we could beat you up, knock you around a bit, but that's a lot of work. Got a friend of yours here who might be able to help."

They pulled his wife, Rosemary, through the front door, one guy on each arm. She had a covid mask on covering duct tape across her mouth. Her face was white as a sheet, and, when she saw her husband, her eyes opened even wider than they were.

"She doesn't know anything!" Aiden screamed. "She can't tell you anything," he added with a whimper. "Just leave her alone. Please, let her go."

The leader smiled, pointing at the woman,

"You're probably right, Sean. She probably doesn't know anything—at least not much. But here's what we're going to do," pausing for a moment, "You're Irish, right?"

"I'm from Ireland, yeah."

"Ever heard of an Irish kneecapping, Sean? Ever heard of one of those?"

Aiden just stood trembling, looking at his wife.

"Well, it's like this, Sean. Someone puts a pistol behind your kneecap—go ahead John—show him." The man pulled a pistol from his belt and held it behind Rosemary's left knee.

"Then they shoot out the kneecap. Doesn't kill you, and nowadays they make pretty good replacement knees—lot of blood, though. Then there's always the second knee." He pulled Sean up by his collar and yelled in his face. "So which knee should we start with on your pretty little wife, Sean? Left . . . or right?"

"Just let her go," Sean gasped. "I'll tell you everything."

So, he told them about the envelope, but claimed he had never opened it and didn't know what was inside. "Whitey told me not to open it, so I didn't. I don't know what's in it." He walked over to the safe, opened it, pulled out the white envelope, and handed it to the guy doing the talking. The man ripped it open and found the key.

"Looks like one of those bank keys," said the one still holding the gun. "Like for a safe deposit box," the other added.

"You sure you don't know the bank, Sean?"

"I didn't even know what was in the envelope. He swore me to secrecy. When I asked him what I was supposed to do with it, he simply said to hold it and I'd know who to give it to, and when." Raising his hands, "I guess that's now. You have it. Do whatever you want with it."

"Sean, you made the right decision just now. We're going to take this key and figure out what it is. Keep one thing in mind, though. We, and others, know who you are and where you are. You open your mouth about this, and that kneecapping might still happen. We clear on that, Sean?"

"I understand."

Turning to his wife, "You understand, Ma'am?" She nodded; her mouth still taped. The men then walked out.

Aiden pulled the tape off Rosemary's mouth and they held each other tight as they sobbed together.

"Is that it, Sean? Is that the last of Whitey Bulger?"

He shook his head, "Probably not. They'll be back."

"Why?" she cried.

"Cause they're not going to be able to get into the damn box without me—it's in my name. And they're probably going to learn that I opened the box two weeks ago. So, they'll be back."

"You did what? How much more don't I know about? Mother of God, Sean. So, what do we do?" She sobbed.

He thought for a moment, looked at her, "Have you seen the news today?"

"You mean about the Gardner Museum?"

"Yeah, the Gardner Museum. We're going to have to call that lady at the museum."

"What the heck does that have to do with us?"

"It's what's in the box, Rose. The Gardner Museum stolen art is in that safe deposit box. Guess it's been there for thirty years—since I got the key. But something is very crazy about the story they're telling. There's no way that eagle they say they got came out of that box. 'Cause I saw it there. Two weeks ago. And I don't think anyone else can get into the box. So, I think we have to call her. I don't know what else to do. She said no one's going to be prosecuted. They just want the art back. And there's the reward. Who knows, maybe we'll qualify for some of the reward."

"Do what you have to, Sean. Just get us out of this mess," she sobbed.

Chapter Thirty-Two

Aiden Calls Mackie

"Gardner Museum, Kathryn Mackie here."

"Miss Mackie, you're the one from the TV news, right?"

"Yes sir, that's me. Who is this?"

"You don't know me Ma'am. Name's Aiden—Sean Aiden. Just listen to me for a second. You gotta know, someone's tricking you." She waived her hand frantically at the two agents sitting in her office wearing ear fobs and mikes. They nodded, moving their hands for her to continue.

"What do you mean?"

"That's not the real eagle you got there—couldn't be—someone gave you a fake!"

"Slow down, sir. We've checked it out pretty thoroughly. Why don't you think it's the real thing?"

"Cause the real thing—the real eagle—it's in a vault in a bank basement in downtown Boston."

"How could that be?"

"Look, Miss Mackie, I saw it with my own eyes two weeks ago. And it sure as hell hasn't flown out of that vault."

"You want to tell me where? Take us there to see the real eagle?"

"Can't do that, Ma'am. That's why I'm calling. I'm in big trouble. Couple of guys just came in here and threatened to kill my wife till I gave them the key to the safe deposit box. I had to give it to them. They just left. I don't have the key anymore."

"Whoa, slow down, Mr. . . . Aiden? Where exactly are you?"

"In my gallery on Second Street in Southie—with my wife—and when these guys find they can't get into the box, they're probably going to come back and kill us—at least kill my wife. We need some help. You said on TV the FBI was involved. I can't trust the police. Maybe I can trust the FBI."

"The FBI is involved, sir, and I think they're moving already to help you . . ." looking across the room, she saw the agents give thumbs up signs. "But where's the bank vault? Where are these guys going?"

"It's the Bank of Boston building—100 Federal Street—but they won't get there right away."

"Why not?"

"Cause they got the key, but they don't know what bank it goes to. It'll take them a while to figure that out. Then they'll go there and still not get in cause they don't know the right name. So, then they'll come back and probably shoot us."

"And why won't they get in at the bank?"

"Cause the damn box is in my name. Twenty-five years ago, Whitey Bulger put the box in my name. And that's where your art is—including the eagle. It's been there the whole time."

An agent crossed the room and slipped a note in front of her, which she read and nodded, "Do you remember the box number, Mr. Aiden?"

"Sort of hard to forget," he answered. "It's box one hundred."

"Okay, Mr. Aiden, just stay where you are. The FBI's on the way. Should be there any minute. They'll help you. I need to see what's going on at the bank. We'll work on that, too. I'm sure we'll talk again," hanging up.

One of the agents in her office was talking in a quiet voice on his phone. She listened.

"Yes, sir. We'll stay here with her. Team one should be at the guy's store. They'll take them to headquarters. . . . Got it. Full protection. Let us know what happens at the bank."

He looked over at Mackie, "You heard that. Everyone's moving. We stay here till we hear from Wilcox."

Chapter Thirty-Three

At the Bank

Special Agent Wilcox called the bank as his car sped across town. Took a while to get through to a person, and then a while longer to a person who was at all helpful. Finally, a vice president came on the line.

"FBI? What's the problem."

"This is Special Agent Jim Wilcox, sir, head of our Boston office. I'm about to pull up to your 100 Federal Street office. Have a team of agents with me. We're headed down to your vault. We think there's a safe deposit box there holding some valuable contraband. We need to secure the area and go over things with someone in charge . . ."

"Are we being robbed?" the man cried.

"No, no. Nothing like that. Calm down, sir. We have everything under control. Just need to make sure no one shows up to get into that box before we get there. I'll be there in less than five minutes."

Security guards were inside the revolving doors when Wilcox and his team entered. They looked quickly at the proffered id's and led the team across the marble floors, down the staircase to the vault.

Vice President Jones and others stood by the massive vault door which led to the safe deposit boxes. He looked more carefully at the identification and badges and placed a call. He evidently received satisfactory confirmation that they were who they claimed. "Okay," he finally said, "what's going on. What do you want to do?"

Wilcox quickly explained that someone had stolen the key to one of the boxes and would probably try to get into the box this afternoon, or, more likely, Monday morning, since it was now after four o'clock. They probably wouldn't know the owner's name, so they'd probably be turned away. The FBI was fairly certain the box contained contraband—stolen goods. Once turned away, he intended to arrest them as they left the bank, recover the key, and return with the real owner to open and inspect the box.

"I'd like to have an agent stationed here—looking like a banker—for additional security. We also need to know from you the name of the box owner and whether it's recently been entered."

"Well, agent, we're not supposed to release that type of information—without a court order of course," the banker responded somewhat primly.

"Look, all I need is the name and the date of last entry. I can get a court order, but if you make me do that, I'll need to bring in our special reaction team, with full body armor and weapons, to close you down and secure the place while we go to court. I'd rather not do that."

The man went white and his eyes dilated as he backed off in shock.

"No, no, we can't do that. It would be a media nightmare." Turning to an assistant, "Do we have the records?"

"Sure. All we need is the box number."

"Box one hundred," said Wilcox.

The assistant went over to a monitor and punched in some numbers, reading the screen.

"Looks like the owner is a Mr. Sean Aiden, and, . . . Jesus Christ, it was opened in 1994 but never entered till two weeks ago. One of the big, thirty-inch deep boxes—only a few of those."

"That's what we'd been told," acknowledged Wilcox. "Everything's adding up. My guess is they'll send in some proper looking front—maybe a lawyer. Although we want him turned away, we want the name and last entry date mentioned to him. Let's sit down and go over some details, Mr. Jones. You could get some real good press out of this. I promise there'll be no disturbance in the bank."

Chapter Thirty-Four

Friday Evening

Kate had sat in her office all afternoon after Aiden's call, waiting nervously for updates. As time went by, she grew increasingly nervous. What was going on?

Finally, at almost five o'clock, Special Agent Wilcox walked in with a tight, but satisfied, smile on his face. "I think we did it, Kate. I think we pulled it off."

"The art?"

"That's probably going to take a couple of more days."

"But . . ." she interrupted.

"I'll explain. Everything has pretty much checked out. We've got Mr. and Mrs. Aiden over at our headquarters, and I think they're telling the truth. We're at the bank, and, sure enough, there is a box one hundred under his name that has sat there unopened for over twenty-five years. Until about two weeks ago when bank records show a Sean Aiden entered the box."

"Did he remove anything?" she cried anxiously.

"We don't know, but he says not, except for this small etching he said he took on impulse." He held out the small two inch square Rembrandt etching that Aiden had removed from the box and today turned over to the FBI.

"Oh my god," she whispered, looking at the piece. "That's one of the pieces taken. Oh my god. We have to get into that box. We have to secure it."

"Slow down, Kate. First, the box is secure. We have agents there, and they'll be there throughout the weekend."

"The weekend!" she yelled. "No, let's get it open now."

"Kate, we're going to wait for someone to show up with the key—probably on Monday."

"Then arrest them and unlock the box?"

"Not quite that easy, Kate. What are we going to arrest them for? And those thugs aren't going to show up. They'll probably send a very respectable front—probably an attorney—with some story about needing to get access for his client. As of right now, we don't have a crime. But if we send them back to Aiden's, which we will, we'll have video and mikes to record everything at his shop. He'll be alone—we'll have his wife protected—and if we get them on tape saying what they said to him before, then we arrest them. Extortion, kidnapping, maybe even for Whitey's murder. They'll be out of the picture, and we'll have the key and Sean Aiden to open the box without incident. But it can't happen before Monday, Kate."

"I guess you're right," she said dejectedly. "I just wanted it finished today. I guess two more days won't hurt. What do we tell everyone?"

"Nothing, Kate. We say nothing. Remember, we still have a scam going on here. A little different from the one you planned, but we have to play it out."

He paused before continuing, "There is one more thing, Kate. Doesn't really involve you, or the museum, but based upon what Mr. Aiden says he was told by these thugs, we now have some confirmation of what some of us at the Bureau have long believed."

"Which is?"

"We think someone high up in Justice, or the FBI, is a mole."

"A mole?"

"Someone has been helping Whitey Bulger for years. He had the Boston FBI office on his payroll. And some in the bureau have thought for years that the taint went higher—all the way to Washington. When Bulger was transferred to the West Virginia prison, that someone probably thought he was about to be outed. So, the transfer was leaked to the general prison population. And guess what happened? Whitey was killed before he revealed anything. And remember, it took us almost twenty years to find him. He might have been getting tips from the inside during those twenty years."

She raised her hands and asked, "So what does that have to do with us—with this operation?"

"Well, right now in Washington, and over the weekend, they're grabbing cell phones from people and administering polygraphs. If we arrest these three thugs on Monday, we'll keep them separate, play one off against the other, and maybe find out a bit more about how the information on Whitey's transfer got out. Remember, for this second-rate stuff they've done in Boston, they face maybe a few years in prison. For killing Bulger in a federal prison, penalty's life—maybe even death. We'll have some leverage over them. So, we think your operation might help us finally get rid of the Whitey Bulger scourge."

"What do you need from us, Jim?"

"Yeah, let's get back to this operation. Make sure some art restorers are working here Monday. If we open the box, we want them to supervise how we handle everything. We'll get them to the bank, and they can accompany the box and its contents to our lab. We'll do a bunch of forensics—don't worry—won't damage anything. Then we'll deliver everything back to you. And you might start thinking about a big homecoming party next week, Kate." He smiled and held out his hand. She brushed it aside and hugged him, saying, "I think we did it, Special Agent Wilcox. We pulled off the scam of the century to solve the biggest robbery in history. And, most important, we got these paintings back where they belong."

Chapter Thirty-Five

Monday Morning

Two FBI agents dropped Aiden at his shop Monday morning, having kept him and Rosemary at a secure hotel location over the weekend. As he entered the shop, things looked the same, but he'd been told about the work performed over the weekend by the FBI. A small, blinking box was now attached to each of the two rear ceiling corners. Barely noticeable, they looked like a standard alarm system. The FBI had assured him that they provided full video and sound surveillance of the entire store. The devices were being monitored by agents in a van parked a block away. At ten thirty his phone rang, displaying a number he knew was the FBI.

"Yes?"

"Okay, Sean, it's started. A guy's at the bank getting a run around about accessing the box. We think you'll have visitors within an hour. Don't worry. We're seconds away."

They stormed in at eleven thirty. The same three as on Friday.

"Why're you guys back? I gave you everything you wanted."

"You gave us shit, Aiden," yelled the same spokesman as Friday. "You went into that bank two weeks ago! Probably emptied the box. We got someone going after that little wife of yours, and she's gonna be history. Next, we'll get your boy. You shouldn't have fucked with us, Mister."

"No, no—I didn't take anything," raising his hands in surrender. I opened it to see what was there, but I didn't take anything."

"Okay, so what was there?" the guy barked.

"The Gardner Museum art. That's what's in the box."

"What the hell's that?! I'm not interested in any fucking art. Where's the cash? Did you grab the fucking cash? Look, Mister, we took care of Whitey, and we'll take care of you and your whole goddamned family if need be." He grabbed a pistol from his belt and slashed it across Aiden's face, driving him to his knees.

"Where's the fucking cash?!"

Six agents barreled in through the front and rear doors, brandishing pistols and yelling,

"On the floor! Now! We're FBI. Drop that pistol and get on the floor—all three of you. Agents, take'em down. Cuff'em. Grab their weapons."

Aiden was on his knees, his hands to his face and dripping blood.

"Thank you," he cried, tears mixing with his blood. "Is it over now? Am I finally out of this mess?"

"Get a medic in here for Mr. Aiden," the lead agent ordered. "Take these three to headquarters; separate cars; separate cells. No calls till Wilcox gets there." Turning to Aiden, "Mr. Aiden, we'll take care of you. Let me look at your face," gently pulling Aiden's hands away from the wound. "It probably hurts like hell, but it's not too bad. Some stitches and you'll be good as new. Remember, we need you to go to the bank with us to get into the box. You okay with that?"

The shopkeeper nodded as he stood and stumbled to his desk chair.

Two FBI agents drove Aiden to the bank. His face bandaged, he had regained some composure. They drove down a steep ramp into the underground parking lot where Special Agent Wilcox was waiting with the key to the safe deposit box. He stood in the garage next to a light armored vehicle and a squad from the FBI's Hostage Rescue Team. Aiden's driver pulled up and rolled down his window.

"Got the whole team, I see."

Wilcox nodded tersely, "Not taking any chances. This guy Whitey held us out to dry for too many years. We're getting this box out of the bank and into this truck and we're getting it back to headquarters. No one's going to interfere. We'll do it quickly, and we're not even going to open it till we have it behind our locked doors and secured."

Looking over at Aiden, "You ready for this? Have your id proving you're Sean Aiden?" Aiden nodded. "Okay. I have the key. They're ready for us inside. In and out quickly. Let's do it."

Things went quickly and smoothly. They sent Aiden home with protection, and in half an hour the FBI team was assembled around the safe deposit box in the FBI lab. They were joined by two art restorers from the Gardner and one who had been borrowed from the Museum of Fine Arts. Before them on a large table sat a gray safe deposit box, twenty inches wide, twenty inches high, thirty inches deep. The hinged top was closed. Wilcox took charge.

"Everyone, gloves on. Everything here is being recorded, so we'll do it slowly and I'll do the narration. We want the FBI technicians to first look for prints and DNA." Looking over to the three restorers, "If you think we're doing anything wrong—anything that will cause any damage—you yell out. Don't be shy. Most important thing here is that we cause no damage." Pointing at an older man next to the box, "Okay, Joe, open it up and let's get started."

The man swung the top up and to the back. On the top was a rolled-up canvas which had been folded over at one end after being rolled to fit into the box. One of the restorers spoke out.

"If that's what I think it is, it's the biggest piece that was taken—Rembrandt's *A Lady and a Gentleman*. That fold could be a real problem if it's been like that for thirty years. Lift it out real carefully but do not unfold it. We'll try to soften the fold with a little moisture and maybe then a hair dryer."

"Okay, Joe, do as she says. Lift it out real careful and put it on the table so they can work on the fold. Looks like it might be the only one folded."

Another restorer added, "Should be the only one. The others are all smaller and should fit in this box rolled. If it was done carefully, the rolling might not have caused any damage."

It took about an hour to remove the art. But there was more than art in the container. On the bottom, in neat, tightly bound packages, were twenty bundles of one hundred dollar bills. They figured it to be a million dollars.

Chapter Thirty-Six

Monday Evening

Special Agent Wilcox, Kate Mackie, and Marilyn Ketchum—the three who had hatched the scheme—met in Ketchum's office to go over the day's events.

"Went pretty much like we thought it would," he said. "A very professional attorney showed up at the bank at ten o'clock to check the safe deposit box of a very important client. He had the key," chuckling, "but he seemed to have some problem with his client's name. He first tried Bulger, and when that struck out, he didn't know quite what to say. As planned, our agent, playing the role of bank clerk, let it slip that a Mr. Sean Aiden had visited the box just a couple of weeks ago. The attorney left in a bit of a huff, and we followed him. He was on his phone soon as he hit the sidewalk."

"Very soon after, a car of thugs showed up at Aiden's shop. It wasn't pleasant, but Aiden played his role perfectly and drew them out to make all sorts of threats against him and his wife. We got it all on video. They talked about having taken care of Whitey and that they'd do the same to him if he didn't cooperate. They hit him with a pistol before we got in and arrested the whole crew, but he's okay."

"We had a warrant all ready for the attorney, and we picked him up with the key and got his phone. We'd like to see who he was calling."

"And," added Ketchum, "we've been told you got into the safe deposit box without incident and recovered everything."

"And in pretty good shape, as I understand," added Mackie. "The larger Rembrandt had been folded over, but everything else was pretty carefully rolled or flat and in decent condition. Even the folded Rembrandt was folded at the bottom of the canvas—if at the top, the fold would have gone right through their faces."

Wilcox continued, "The eagle was there, too. We're finished with the art, and we'll deliver it back whenever you want. We also found quite a bit of cash in the box. We got Whitey's prints on the inside of the box, on the cash, and maybe his DNA."

"How much cash?" asked Mackie.

"Looks like a million bucks."

"And who gets that?" she asked.

"Good question. That's for the lawyers to fight over. I think there are claims against his estate, and maybe his family has a claim, and, who knows, maybe the museum can claim it for the loss of its art for thirty years. Don't really know who'll get the cash."

Mackie looked at Wilcox, shaking her head, "So what the hell happened back in 1994, before he disappeared? Why'd Whitey do this?"

Wilcox answered, "I think he knew during his last few years that his days were numbered. He had accumulated a lot of cash. The experts say in the millions. He had even split a questionable fourteen million dollar lottery jackpot with his buddies in 1991. He knew the guys who pulled off the Gardner job and knew they couldn't sell the stuff. It was too hot. So, he took it off their hands for probably a lot less than even its discounted value and put it on ice for the future. Just before he disappeared, he decided to use Sean Aiden, who had shown himself to be easily manipulated and, in his own way, trustworthy."

"So, how'd he keep this box for so many years," Ketchum queried.

"That's an easy one. It was a big box—rent was one thousand dollars a year. He paid the bank twenty-five thousand dollars up front for twenty-five years."

"But it's been more than twenty-five years, hasn't it?"

"That, we haven't quite figured out," Wilcox said. "Just before the twenty-five years expired, someone sent in payment for another five years. And they sent the right amount, even though the rent had increased. So, someone had checked with the bank. We have no idea who. That would have been in 2019, after he was killed. Someone knew something about this box. Someone who survived him. But they didn't have the key till they found Aiden."

"And who do you think made that call to Aiden Thursday night," asked Ketchum.

"Oh, we think we know who made the call, Ma'am. Nothing illegal about making a call and asking a few questions. We'll never connect that caller to these thugs we arrested. Too many layers of separation. Same thing with the lawyer who went to the bank. He's in the Boston elite—maybe even on your Board. Won't get anything from him. But we have the three thugs in custody. We're still adding up the charges against them. They won't see daylight for some years. We now also have some good leads on who in Washington was helping Whitey Bulger over the years. Keep your ears open to hear about an early retirement at the Justice Department."

"One more thing before we finish here," said Kate's boss. "Kate, you pulled this off, almost on your own—certainly it was your plan. The FBI can't get rewards, but you can, and I think you should. I've talked to the Board, and although a final decision hasn't been made, I think you're going to get that reward."

"Oh my god," exclaimed Mackie. "I hadn't exactly forgotten about the reward, but, . . . I don't know what to say."

Wilcox spoke up. "I should mention, ladies, that Mr. Aiden has already raised the same question. He did make the call to the museum. So, the reward might end up being split in some way between the two of you."

"Will he go along with that?" Mackie asked.

Wilcox looked at her, "He won't have much choice. He was up to his ears in Whitey's stuff, and his name was on the account. He's fairly well thought of around Southie. We could indict him and ruin him, even if we don't eventually convict him of anything. I'm pretty sure he'll go along with what we recommend."

"And my final question, before we all go out and celebrate," Mackie said. What about my eagle? I told the professor that I'd try to get it back to him for him to recover the value of the gold."

"Don't know what you're talking about, Miss Mackie," Wilcox said, as he picked up a case that had been at his feet and placed it next to her desk. "Only eagle we know about is back home at the museum. There's only one golden eagle."

EPILOGUE

Two weeks later, Mackie read in the Globe that the highest and longest serving career employee at the Department of Justice had suddenly left the department for health reasons. No further explanation was given. Then she received a call from Wilcox:

"Read about the early retirement, Kate?"

"Yes, I saw it. Just pushed him out, right? Nothing more?"

"It would have been impossible to prove much. It is past history. So, we buried it. But as far as nothing more, we are putting together a task force to see if there's more cash stashed away out there."

"How you gonna do that," she asked.

"We're going to start with a survey of all the banks in the Boston area with safe deposit boxes. We're looking for boxes opened before 1995 and not entered since then. If we find any, we might find more of his cash."

"Great idea, Jim! And, I don't know if you've heard, but they've agreed to the reward payments—six million to me and four to Mr. Aiden. They were insistent that he lose some and not participate equally because of his past conduct. He's agreed."

"That's terrific, Kate. This mean an early retirement for you, too?"

"No, probably not. Taxes will take a big bite of it, and, at least for now, I enjoy the job. Anyway, I'm too young to retire. But, I do have some personal news . . ."

"Which is?"

"Which is, I'm going to get married! I got a diamond on my finger, and Jonathon hopes to be transferred to his Firm's Boston office. So don't be surprised if you get an invitation to a wedding."

"I'm very happy for you, Kate. And I'll be there."

The same day, she took a call from the Fort Meyers 239 exchange.

"Professor—this you?"

"Sure is, Kate. Want to thank you for the package."

"You more than earned it, Professor. Has it disappeared?"

"Just as I promised—it's gone. But I do have one question."

"Yes?"

"I examined it pretty carefully, and I noticed some shaving off the bottom. Thought you had said the testing didn't do any damage. Just wondering . . ."

"Very observant, professor. No, that wasn't from the testing. I shaved a small strip of gold off the base—just enough for two wedding bands. Let's keep that our little secret, okay?"

"No problem, Kate. Guess we have a few secrets to keep."

AUTHOR'S NOTE

Whitey Bulger terrorized South Boston for many years, and the nearby Gardner Museum theft did occur and remains unsolved. Beyond that, this book is a work of fiction and of the author's imagination. The eagle was said to be bronze, but it's never come back, and, as the Kingston Trio sang many years ago,

. . . And his fate is still unlearned
He may ride forever
'Neath the streets of Boston
He's the man, who never returned.

CPSIA information can be obtained
at www.ICGtesting.com
Printed in the USA
JSHW040709220523
42039JS00001B/1